P9-BZT-082

DISCARD

DATE DUE

BRODART, CO.   Cat. No. 23-221

THE SHAPE OF
THE WORLD
TO COME

THE SHAPE OF THE

CHARTING THE GEOPOLITICS OF A NEW CENTURY

WORLD TO COME

LAURENT COHEN-TANUGI

TRANSLATED BY GEORGE HOLOCH

COLUMBIA UNIVERSITY PRESS

NEW YORK

COLUMBIA UNIVERSITY PRESS

Publishers Since 1893
New York   Chichester, West Sussex
Guerre ou paix copyright © 2007 Éditions Grasset et Fasquelle
Copyright © 2008 Columbia University Press

All rights reserved

Library of Congress Cataloging-in-Publication Data

Cohen-Tanugi, Laurent, 1957–
    [Guerre ou paix. English]
    The shape of the world to come : charting the geopolitics of
a new century / Laurent Cohen-Tanugi; translated by George Holoch.
        p. cm.
    Includes bibliographical references and index.
    ISBN 978-0-231-14600-5 (cloth : alk. paper)—ISBN 978-0-231-51790-4 (e-book)
    1. Geopolitics—21st century. 2. Globalization. I. Title.

JC319.C64   2008
327.1001—DC22

                                              2008001455

∞

Casebound editions of Columbia University Press books are
printed on permanent and durable acid-free paper.

Printed in the United States of America

c 10 9 8 7 6 5 4 3 2 1

References to Internet Web Sites (URLs) were accurate at the
time of writing. Neither the author nor Columbia University
Press is responsible for Web sites that may have expired or
changed since the book was prepared.

ACC LIBRARY SERVICES
AUSTIN, TX

TO MY PARENTS AND
TO THEIR GRANDCHILDREN

BUT, AFTER ALL, SHADOWS
THEMSELVES ARE BORN OF LIGHT.
AND ONLY HE WHO HAS EXPERIENCED
DAWN AND DUSK, WAR AND PEACE,
ASCENT AND DECLINE, ONLY HE
HAS TRULY LIVED.

— STEFAN ZWEIG —

THE WORLD OF YESTERDAY, 1941

CONTENTS

PREFACE   *xi*

ACKNOWLEDGMENTS   *xv*

INTRODUCTION: THE WORLD IS NOT FLAT   *1*

1   THE NEW FACE OF GLOBALIZATION   *5*

2   THE END OF THE ATLANTIC ERA   *27*

3   THE GEOPOLITICS OF GLOBALIZATION   *51*

4   THE WEST ON TRIAL   *73*

5   THE WEAPONS OF PEACE   *93*

CONCLUSION: SHAPING THE WORLD TO COME   *115*

NOTES   *119*

INDEX   *123*

PREFACE

This book was born from an intuition and a worry.

First the intuition, felt as early as September 11, 2001: after the care-free interlude of the first post–cold war decade, we have entered a world far more uncertain than that of the second half of the twentieth century. This feeling is now widely shared, but the terrorist threat has tended to obscure other aspects of this change of global paradigm that are just as important. Next the worry: it has to do precisely with the distance separating this multifarious reality from the perception we have of it, the gap between the vertiginous speed at which our environment is being transformed and the slowness of reactions inherent in democratic societies.

Gaps of this kind are as common in international relations as in private affairs. At the outset of the 1990s, at the peak of European unification, the political failings leading to the crisis Europe is going through today were already discernible. Similarly, ten years later, while transatlantic relations grew poisonous on the eve of the American invasion of Iraq, the objective factors for closer relations between Europe and America were already at work. Today again, the illusion of the peaceful homogenization of the planet through globalization—a legacy of the halcyon days after the end of the cold war—continues to conceal from us the fact that that very globalization has become the most powerful force for change in world geopolitics, for better and for worse.

On the one hand, recent statistics on the diminution in the number of wars and deaths caused by conflict since the end of the confrontation between East and West[1] should not make us forget that conflict has above all changed its nature—with terrorism, civil wars, nonstate actors—and that the future carries new threats and the certainty of large-scale geopolitical upheavals. On the other, the emergence of new centers of economic power outside the Western sphere is also a great opportunity for considerable segments of the world's population, with globalization a source of enrichment for all humanity, including the industrial West.

The global reshaping we are witnessing nevertheless requires vigilance on the part of the Western democracies; it will inevitably translate into a reduction of their influence over world affairs and even over their own domestic situations to the benefit of other powers and other value systems. And, while no civilization is a priori incompatible with democracy and humanistic values, only the West places freedom, tolerance, the separation of politics and religion, and the primacy of the individual at the center of its view of the world. It cannot, unless it denies itself, renounce the universal nature of those values and their defense for the common good wherever they are threatened by new forms of totalitarianism.

Things were simpler in this respect in the cold war period: the "free world" and Communist totalitarianism were in open confrontation, and other civilizations were not likely to constitute a threat to the democratic West. In the world taking shape before our eyes, no nation is officially the enemy of any other, but power is disseminated, yesterday's adversaries and today's "partners" have not really adopted political freedom and democracy, while new forms of totalitarianism in religious guise are coming to light.

Neither alarmist, nor even necessarily pessimistic, this book expresses a Western point of view, open to global change and welcoming greater diversity, to which we must adapt, but intent on seeing the democratic world maintain meaningful influence and ultimate strategic superiority in the twenty-first century. This bias might be considered conservative: from my perspective it has more to do with simple self-awareness and the instinct for survival of liberty and other essential Western values.

I will conclude with a few methodological considerations.

This book aims to offer and submit for debate a global, synthetic, and predictive vision of tomorrow's world, obviously one that is not exhaustive. Each piece in this kaleidoscope has given rise to a wealth of literature to which the reader may refer and with which I have no claim of competing. As for the predictive aspect, it is naturally nourished by knowledge and analysis of the present and favors certain hypotheses: a linear development of the rise of China stands out as the most decisive and the most uncertain among them.

These limitations, inherent in any exercise of this kind, do not excuse us from the duty of analysis and anticipation incumbent on any political community intent on maintaining control over its own fate.

ACKNOWLEDGMENTS

The original French edition of this book benefited from to the help of Julia Cagé, a student in economics at the École Normale Supérieure in Paris, whose research and critical mind have stimulated my thinking, as from the valuable suggestions of a virtual reading committee consisting of Gilles Chouraqui, my French publisher Olivier Nora, Katherine Rubinski, and Jodie and Pierre Cohen-Tanugi. It is even more indebted to the unfailing devotion of my assistants Anna Woods-Bertasi and Delphine Qui, both admitted on this occasion into the very exclusive fellowship of interpreters of my hieroglyphics.

The English-language edition, based on George Holoch's excellent translation, has been reviewed and updated by the author and benefited from Ann Pollock's and Jodie Cohen-Tanugi's insightful comments.

To all of them as well as to the countless involuntary contributors to these reflections, to the Columbia University Press team for its professionalism and enthusiasm, and to my family for its divine patience I express my deepest gratitude.

THE SHAPE OF
THE WORLD
TO COME

INTRODUCTION

THE WORLD IS NOT FLAT

The post–cold war era has come to an end.

Less than fifteen years after the fall of the iron curtain, an event full of hope, the twenty-first century has begun by plunging us into a much more uncertain world, one that promises to be with us for some time. This book aims to explore this new world, sometimes hailed as "multipolar" in contrast to the preceding period of unipolar American power.

By the end of the 1980s the geopolitics of the planet had already experienced a major paradigm shift with the end of the Soviet-American confrontation that had been the organizing principle of international relations since 1945. In many respects the fall of the Berlin Wall on November 9, 1989, swiftly followed by the implosion of the Soviet empire, German reunification, and the reunification of the European continent, tolled the death knell for the bipolar world and the international system of the second half of the twentieth century, in turn generating a succession of profound transformations. However, what has since then become known as the post–cold war era will probably remain as an epilogue to the past century rather than a prelude to the new one. This has less to do with the calendar than with the fact that the decade of the 1990s that embodied that era now looks like a euphoric and illusory parenthesis, the symbol of a bygone golden age, brutally closed by the attacks of September 11, 2001.

In the West the period following the cold war was marked by the utopian vision of the end of history, which was trumpeted as the result of the global ideological victory of democracy and capitalism. This was illustrated by a series of favorable developments: the triumph of the American model embodied in the Internet revolution and the "new economy," the progress of European unification, the Israeli-Palestinian peace process begun with the Oslo agreement, the hopes for quick democratization in Russia, the promise of a "new international order" expressed by George Bush in 1990. The prospect confronting us after the shock of September 11, 2001, has a much darker aspect, and it is bound to last much longer. The historical significance of the events of that date will long be the subject of ideological debate. It will be used here primarily as a symbolic marker for a changing world. As the tragic dimension of history embodied in the haunting images of the Twin Towers collapsing tore apart the liberal illusion of prosperity and democracy for all promised by globalization and the technological revolution, a series of historical developments since then have laid out the geopolitical outlines of the beginning new century.

The first of these has been the emergence of radical Islam as a destabilizing force in the international system, whether in the form of terrorism, the growth of fundamentalism in the Arab-Muslim world, the collapse of hope for peace between Israel and the Palestinians, and the instrumentalization of Islam for the benefit of ambitions for regional, if not global, power. These developments and their menacing consequences continue to dominate the international agenda and have darkened our horizon while masking other, even more significant changes.

The spectacular entry of China onto the international stage, symbolized by its admission, also in 2001, to the World Trade Organization, was another striking signal heralding the advent of a new era. Underway since the late 1970s, the awakening of the Chinese giant, with its multiple economic and geopolitical repercussions, has become an inescapable reality thirty years later. In its wake have come other emerging powers, such as India and Russia, and strategic earthquakes that we have barely begun to feel.

The sometimes troubling rise to power of these new actors has coincided with a parallel weakening of the two major centers of the Western world, symbolized on one hand by the failure of the American adventure in Iraq and on the other by the rejection of the European constitutional treaty in the spring of 2005. The American intervention in Iraq, a highly questionable result of the September 11 attacks, has had devastating effects on the credibility and prestige of the United States and on its freedom of action in the world, particularly in the Middle East. It has affected both transatlantic relations and the progress of European unification. The French and Dutch rejection of the European Union (EU) constitutional treaty, a symptom rather than a cause of a profound crisis of the European political project, not only deepened that crisis but also reduced the capacity of the EU and its member states to influence the coming new world. Moreover, it significantly weakened the European unification project, which had represented a key advance in postwar international relations. The outcome of these developments taken together marks the end of what may be called the Atlantic era, characterized by shared leadership of America and Europe over the international system, which the defeat of Communism should have reinforced.

In contrast to the post–cold war period and that of Soviet-American détente, which beginning in the 1970s preceded the fall of the iron curtain, the multipolar world on the horizon will not be the balanced and harmonious system that some in Europe and in the developing world posed as an alternative to the "American Empire." It is in fact characterized by a return of conflict, assertions of nationalism and identity, competition for energy resources, and power politics in a world previously dominated by the spread of economic and political liberalism and multilateralism, factors leading to peace and diminished roles for power strategies and sovereignty in international relations. This does not mean that the major trends of the preceding period—economic globalization, technological revolution, regional integration, demo-

cratic progress—are no longer at work. Quite the contrary, globalization has emerged as the main driving force of the international system. It now, however, coexists in a complex dynamic with traditional
geopolitics, which, by a paradoxical reversal, it has itself helped to revive. These conflicting tendencies are likely to remain inextricably in-
tertwined, creating an ambivalent world in which it will be necessary
to play on two realms: the realm of economic integration and multilateralism, that is, liberal, "postmodern" internationalism, by definition
peaceful and astrategic; and the more traditional, perhaps even regressive, realm of confrontation between national and regional strategies
of power against a background of terrorism, civil wars, and nuclear
proliferation.

Contrary to Thomas Friedman's optimistic vision of a world "flattened" by the virtues of globalization, the sustainability and positive
outcome of that coexistence are far from guaranteed.[1] Between integration and fragmentation, nationalism and multilateralism, dialogue
and clash of civilizations, war and peace, the shape of the world to
come will depend to a great degree on the use the new economic giants make of their power and on the ability of Western democracies
to preserve their dynamism, their cohesion, and their influence for the
common good.

In a context of rapid strategic changes, the implications of which
are unpredictable, this book ventures into the new century to decipher
its main driving forces and to offer an interpretative framework that
may serve as a guide for reflection and action. Beyond their geopolitical
effects, are the redistribution of economic power and the widespread
revival of various forms of nationalism and fundamentalism likely to
upset the strategic balance of the planet and the functioning of international society or even to threaten our democracies and our freedoms? If
so, how can the West avert these dangers?

1

THE NEW FACE OF GLOBALIZATION

The twenty-first century's beginning brought some good news and some bad news.

The good news was the long-awaited economic takeoff of a group of emerging nations—China, India, Brazil, and a number of others—and the consequent escape from poverty for hundreds of millions of people. After decades of stagnation and misery, globalization and the conversion to capitalism finally enabled large segments of the third world to begin to flourish, a development holding enormous promise for the disadvantaged majority of mankind. The emerging countries are now driving world growth, positively affecting even the poorest countries of Africa and Asia, while simultaneously offering new opportunities to the most prosperous economies of the planet.

The bad news is the danger of a latent but enduring conflict between the Arab-Muslim world and the West, which has already taken on concrete form in the advent of mass terrorism and calls for jihad, the growth of radical Islamism and extremism in a large number of traditionally moderate and Western-leaning countries, the Iranian nuclear threat, and the increasing frequency of well-orchestrated philosophical and religious disputes between the two civilizations.

Whereas the real depth of this new conflict between East and West remains uncertain, the same thing is not true of the astonishing economic growth of China, India, and several other major countries of the developing world, which will unquestionably change the global balance of power over the course of the next half century. Definitely promising for mankind as a whole, the good news thus also represents a challenge with significant geopolitical implications.

THE RETURN OF HISTORY

While radically different in their nature and consequences, these two developments in opposite directions, which were initiated in the late 1970s by the Chinese shift to modernization, on the one hand, and the Islamic revolution in Iran, on the other, nevertheless share at least three characteristics justifying their status as signposts of a new geopolitical paradigm. They have, in the first place, for better or for worse, propelled onto the front of the world stage, alongside the United States, Europe, and other major industrialized countries, new major non-Western actors. This is a first since the advent of the modern age in the mid nineteenth century, dominated first by Europe then by the North Atlantic world as a whole, and, in this sense, represents a historic break. The historical dimension of this change is even more striking in light of the return of China and India to positions of power on the international stage, not to mention the resurgence of radical Islam hostile to the West, which taken together seem to have projected us several centuries back into the past. In 1820, at the dawn of the industrial revolution, China accounted for about 30 percent of the world economy, India about 15 percent, compared to 23 percent for Europe, and less than 2 percent for the United States. By the middle of the twentieth century, the two Asian giants together accounted for only 8.7 percent of the world economy, which was dominated by the United States (27.3 percent) and Europe (26.3 percent).[1]

These two developments are, moreover, closely tied to globalization. This observation hardly needs elaboration as concerns the economic growth of emerging nations, a direct consequence of the liberalization of world trade. It is more problematic when it comes to establishing a causal link between globalization and the rise of Islamism. This is even more the case when Islamist terrorism is presented as a reaction, however condemnable, to "American globalization." Some experts of the Arab-Muslim world nonetheless expressly assert the existence of such a connection and view terrorism and political Islamism as merely extreme forms of a revival of Islam having to do primarily with religion and cultural identity. They see this revival in turn as induced by the economic and cultural "violence" that Western globalization has inflicted on Arab-Muslim societies.[2] This blurring of the line between religious revival and terrorism is open to challenge, and the current situation of the Arab-Muslim world can no doubt be attributed to many factors other than globalization. It is nonetheless likely that the destabilizing effects on national identity and the social fabric that globalization has produced in the West have been even greater in Islamic societies.

Finally, and most important, these two historical turning points associated with globalization have in turn unseated the international paradigm that, from the 1980s on, even before the fall of the Berlin Wall, and through September 11, 2001, had replaced the bipolar world of the cold war. This period was characterized by an acceleration of economic globalization, worldwide spread of the market economy and the rule of law, the technological revolution, a reduction in power politics and geopolitical tensions, and unchallenged Western leadership. Contrary to what the current rise of protectionist temptations might lead one to suspect, the change of paradigm inaugurated on the ruins of the World Trade Center does not announce a brake on globalization itself. In fact, globalization is flourishing, redefining the balance of economic power throughout the world. In 2006, for instance, the world economy experienced its strongest growth since the oil shock of 1973, and international trade has continued to grow at a rate of 5 to 6 percent per year. Yet, the conjunction of tensions between Islam and the West and the awakening of major countries of the developing world has laid the groundwork for a new world environment in which the geopolitical dimension, security and energy concerns, governments, nationalism, and power strategies are making a strong comeback onto the global economic scene. This is yet another historical turning point and a reversal of perspective, the implications of which we will revert to.

A NEW EAST/WEST CONFLICT?

Awareness of the epochal change we are discussing first arose in the United States on September 11, 2001, when the al Qaeda attacks, seen on live television around the world, brutally connected the unreal and far off chaos of Taliban Afghanistan to the daily life of the world's superpower and billions of individuals in the West and beyond. This dramatic event transformed mass terrorism from virtual to actual reality and demonstrated that Western democracies, no matter how prosperous and powerful, were henceforth unable to isolate themselves from the violent conflicts going on in the Middle East and Central Asia, as they had been doing since 1945, when the great powers exported their own conflicts into proxy wars. On September 11, 2001, security and strategic concerns tragically stormed onto the stage of globalization.

Seven years after this unprecedented act of war on American soil, terrorism of Islamist origin remains the principal threat against the West and hence the most concrete embodiment of the conflict between radical Islam and modernity. But the roots of this conflict, a geopolitical signpost of the opening of a new century, are deeper and more complex than the terrorist threat itself. The appearance of Islamist terrorism in international politics goes back well before September 11, 2001, to the 1979 proclamation of the Islamic Republic of Iran following Ayatollah Khomeini's fundamentalist revolution and the long American hostage crisis that followed. In December of that year the Red Army invaded neighboring Afghanistan, provoking an Islamic resistance that contributed to the defeat of the USSR ten years later. During the course of the 1980s, Shiite fundamentalist control of Iran, the Iran-Iraq war, and the Soviet occupation of Afghanistan led Saudi Arabia and Pakistan to encourage, as a counterweight and with the cooperation of the United

States, a radicalization of Sunni Islam that gave rise to al Qaeda. The implosion of the Soviet Union twelve years after the invasion, followed by the easing of tensions between the United States and Iran, turned the Sunni Islamist movements coming out of Afghanistan, Pakistan, and Saudi Arabia against the United States, and they attempted to seize power in Arab states they considered ungodly.

The new antagonism between Islam and the West is thus inextricably bound up with political and religious conflicts within Islam—between Sunnis and Shiites and, among Sunnis, between fundamentalism and modernity—which instrumentalize it. The denunciation of Israel, of America, and of the West as a whole is in fact primarily a very effective way of winning over the "Arab street" in order to dominate Islam and the Middle East. Although the seizure of power by the Iranian mullahs has remained an isolated phenomenon in the Arab-Muslim world, the 1979 revolution propagated a fundamentalist vision of Islam, inaugurated the practice of suicide attacks, and fostered the emergence of increasingly powerful political pressures on most moderate Arab regimes. Whereas, in the late 1990s, most experts observed that Islamist movements had failed to come to power in the Sunni world,[3] the growth of fundamentalism in many Arab countries since the Iranian revolution has increased with the rise to power of al Qaeda and its historic victory over the American "Great Satan" on September 11, 2001. Since the collapse of the Oslo peace process between Israel and Palestine and the US-led intervention in Iraq, Islamism has become a major political force in the Arab-Muslim world. It has "democratically" taken power in Turkey and Palestine, it threatens the stability of several strategically located countries of the Mediterranean (Morocco), the Middle East (Egypt, Saudi Arabia), and Central Asia (Pakistan), and it fosters chaos in "failed" states such as Afghanistan, Somalia, Sudan, and now Iraq.

The progress of radicalism in the Islamic world carries many stakes that are of critical importance to the international community: security in the face of new threats, the stability and cooperation of nations strategically crucial for the world's geopolitical balance and economic growth, energy supplies, the future of Israel, and the harmonious co-existence with immigrant populations, particularly in Europe. The rise of fundamentalist movements has intensified the clash with modernity in the Arab-Muslim world, but it has also made it more difficult for the fifteen or twenty million Muslims of Europe—a population expected to double by 2025—to integrate and has further intensified the general conflict of values between Islam and the West, which was blown out of proportion by the organized violence of the demonstrations through-out the Islamic world against the Danish cartoons of the Prophet Muhammad. Most important, the danger of a generalized clash between Islam and the West is now heightened by an increasing and deliberately fostered amalgamation of diverse antagonisms that had previously been separate and distinct.

President Bush in his first term played no small role in this "global-ization," by declaring total war on Islamist "terror," creating an artificial link between al Qaeda and the regime of Saddam Hussein to justify American intervention in Iraq, placing ancestral enemies—Persian and Shiite Iran and Iraq under Sunni domination—on the same "axis of evil," and even by articulating the positive, but also globalizing, concept of a "new Middle East." But it would be unfair not to recall that Washington has always distinguished between Islamism and Islam, and that the revival of the historic conflict between Islam and the West has, on the other hand, been at the heart of the strategy of al Qaeda and the international jihadi movement from the outset. Their perspective brings together on one side the "Jews," "Crusaders," and other West-erners, along with their Arab collaborators of every nationality, and on the other the oppressed Muslim populations of Palestine, Iraq, Saudi Arabia, Chechnya, Bosnia, and Afghanistan, regardless of sectarian al-legiance. The danger of current developments lies in the fact that this "globalization" is not any longer merely a matter of political staging but is gradually becoming part of geopolitical reality.

Not so long ago, it was possible to distinguish schematically among five major arenas of conflict involving segments of the West and the

Arab-Muslim world: the Israeli-Palestinian conflict, the total war between al Qaeda and America, soon broadened to the West as a whole,
including Russia, the conflict between the Iraqi "resistance" and American occupation forces, the standoff between Iran and the international
community on the nuclear issue, and, finally, a complex of ideological and religious tensions between Islam and modernity, involving Europe—a secular destination for Muslim immigration—more than the
United States, which is simultaneously more religious and more liberal
than the Old Continent.

However, as these different conflicts have evolved, their successful
instrumentalization by Islamist movements to dramatize a purported
global confrontation between Islam and the West has established dangerous bridges between them. Thanks to the elimination of Saddam
Hussein's Sunni regime and the weakening of Lebanon's sovereignty
have enabled Iran to become involved through proxy fighters in both the
Iraqi civil war and the Lebanese conflict, thereby strengthening its position in the nuclear negotiations with the West. The deterioration of the
Iraqi situation and the summer 2006 war between Israel and Hezbollah
have been direct consequences of this reinforcement of the Iranian position. Similarly, the assumption of power by Hamas in the Palestinian
territories has consolidated the long-standing link between the Israeli-
Palestinian conflict and Islamist terrorism and created new forms of
solidarity. Even more seriously, these developments have brought Arab
public opinion closer to organizations that the international community officially considers to be terrorist (al Qaeda, Hamas, Hezbollah), and
the progress of Islamism in the Arab-Muslim world as a whole is fostering ever more frequent and acute crises between radicalized Islam and
Western culture, particularly in European societies, which are more
secular and irreligious than the United States. The dispute over wearing
veils in school in France, the political exploitation of the Danish cartoons, and the international tension provoked by Pope Benedict XVI's
speech in Regensburg in September 2006 are all illustrations of this drift
toward the dreaded "clash of civilizations." The danger for both camps

is clear: it is the gradual blurring of the crucial dividing line between Islam and Islamism, between political support for any given cause and terrorism, which is likely to give increasing reality to the sense of a global antagonism that is largely artificial.

The operations of transnational Arabic media and the emergence of "Islamic finance" have inevitably contributed, because of the ambiguity of their relationship to fundamentalism, if not terrorism, to the representation of a single Islamic world in which important lines of demarcation are dangerously eroding. The great beneficiary of this attempt to bring the Arab-Muslim world together around a militant fundamentalist line, against the backdrop of widespread chaos in Gaza, Iraq, and Afghanistan, has so far been the Islamic Republic of Iran, with its historic ambition to become a regional power destined to dominate the Middle East and Central Asia.

THE EMERGING WORLD'S REVOLUTION

While America after September 11 and most of the rest of the world in its wake concentrated their energies on the fight against terrorism, an entirely different phenomenon of a much larger scope was quietly developing: the restructuring of world economic hierarchies in favor of China, India, and other emerging countries. The repercussions of this development on the geopolitical configuration of the planet will in the end be much more revolutionary, destabilizing, and, it is to be hoped, positive than the rise of Islamism.

After a century and a half of underdevelopment and marginalization, from the industrial revolution in the West in the nineteenth century up to the last third of the twentieth, the reemergence of China and India as major economic players on the world stage has transformed the geopolitical landscape, with consequences probably even more significant than those produced by Germany's rise to power in the nineteenth century and that of the United States in the twentieth. This development has been reinforced by the rise of other large emerging countries in Eastern Europe (Russia) and in Latin America (Brazil, Mexico), along with South Korea and South Africa. According to the famous BRIC study—for Brazil, Russia, India, and China—by Goldman Sachs, the economies of the four leading emerging countries might surpass those of the old industrialized countries before 2050, as a result of much higher real growth than in Europe and the United States and of the improvement of their macroeconomic fundamentals.[4] More generally, the emerging countries, which in 2006 accounted for about 30 percent of world gross domestic product (about twice as much as in 1980) and more than 80 percent of the world's population, might account for as much as 60 percent of world GDP in 2050. During the last few years, the dynamism of the world economy has also benefited the poorest countries of South Asia and Africa, some of which have recorded growth rates of 10 percent, while the flow of private capital to emerging and developing countries reached a record level of nearly 500 billion dollars in 2005. The twenty-first century will hence witness a remarkable readjustment of the world economy to the benefit of emerging countries, particularly in Asia, and a significant reduction in the gap between demographic weight and wealth around the world.

The rapid rise of new major global or regional economic powers, with China and India in the first rank, is a direct consequence of globalization and its most spectacular contribution to mankind as a whole. The expansion of international commerce in connection with the liberalization of trade and investment flows, a deliberate policy of open borders, a huge low-cost workforce, and an abundance of liquidity in the world economy resulting from a long period of low interest rates finally allowed the awakening of the two Asian giants, and, thanks to a growth rate of 10 percent in China and 6 percent in India over the last twenty years, the access of hundreds of millions of people to a huge middle class able to consume and to save. The accusation that trade liberalization has benefited only rich countries is thus obsolete, which is perhaps not unrelated to the recent weakening of the antiglobalization movement. In fact, thanks to the remarkable speed of its economic growth, Asia has now replaced America as the embodiment of the threat posed by liberal globalization to the old societies of Europe. Europeans and Americans are gradually becoming aware of the fact that globalization means a massive redistribution of economic power and wealth on a worldwide scale to the benefit of countries with large populations, endowed with low-cost labor forces or with natural resources, among which China, India, and, to a lesser degree, Russia, Brazil, the oil states of the Gulf, and South Africa, will be the first to profit.

China, India, Russia, and Brazil share one major asset that is a source of their extraordinary potential: they are "continental nations." These four large countries have territories of continental scale: China and India together have a population of 2.4 billion, and Russia and Brazil possess vast and precious natural resources, particularly in the realm of energy. Each of these economies represents a huge domestic market capable of forming a basis for domestic growth as well as attracting foreign investment. These are the assets that enabled these countries to take full advantage of globalization through the growth of their exports and the inflow of international capital.

But the strength of these new giants of the world economy also comes from a political factor: these continentwide economies are also nations with illustrious histories whose desire to recover influence in the world and whose feeling of national pride can easily be mobilized by their political leaders. This is so because their political regimes are characterized by active state intervention, and, in the case of China and Russia, authoritarianism derived from their imperial and Communist legacies. Moreover—another legacy of Communism (or socialism in India's case)—their economies are still, for the most part, state run. Most large Chinese enterprises are owned or controlled by the state or other political bodies or public entities. Vladimir Putin's Russia has renationalized and concentrated, under tight Kremlin control, the strategic enterprises that Boris Yeltsin privatized in the 1990s, particularly in the oil and gas sector. Even when it does not directly control the capital of business enterprises, the state runs the national economy as a whole to serve the eminently political purpose of a return to power on the international stage.

Honor to whom honor is due: because of its size, its population, and its ambitions, China is on the way to becoming the new global economic superpower. Its industrialization may be compared to European and Japanese reconstruction after the Second World War. Initiated in 1978 with Deng Xiao Ping's "four modernizations"—industry, science, agriculture, and defense—the awakening of the Chinese giant was exclusively oriented toward an opening to the world economy, exploitation of the extraordinary competitive advantage of an abundant low-cost labor force, and importation of foreign capital and technology on a huge scale. The "workshop of the world" in an ever growing and more sophisticated range of manufactured products—from textiles initially to high technology military equipment—the Chinese economy has had an annual growth rate of nearly 10 percent for three decades, based on exports, foreign investment (since 2003 China has been the largest recipient of direct foreign investment), and a national savings rate without equivalent in the developed countries. In 2007 it became the third largest economy in the world, surpassing Germany, and its gross domestic product may surpass that of its neighbor and rival Japan in 2030, and that of the primary world power, the United States, whose enormous deficits it finances, within thirty years. Its entry into the WTO in December 2001 consecrated its integration into the world economy and fostered its adherence to the multilateral system and to the norms of the market economy.

The rise to power of the Middle Kingdom is the outcome of a voluntarist strategy fostered by the authoritarianism of the domestic political regime and the opportunism of Chinese leaders in their acceptance of global capitalism. The availability of a huge, solvent, and rapidly growing market has made China a powerful force able to impose technical standards on multinational companies around the world and to demand from them technology transfers in strategic industries such as nuclear energy, electronics, and transportation.[5] Its export earnings, the abundance of foreign capital, and a national savings rate equivalent to 50 percent of GDP (more than five times the American rate) enable it to invest massively in all areas, including research and development. According to the OECD, in 2006 China became the second largest investor in R&D in the world (136 billion dollars), surpassing Japan (130 billion), and leaving far behind each of the principal economies of the European Union (230 billion for the 15 EU members together). Only the United States remains ahead with 330 billion dollars, but Beijing is striving to match that by 2020.

China's enormous size and its feverish growth rate are having huge effects on key parameters of the world economy, from the increase in oil and raw materials prices caused by its demand to the radical transformation of the international division of labor produced by its low wages and the flood of its cheap exports throughout the world. The resulting massive trade surpluses with the United States and other developed countries, as well as the flow of foreign investment, have made China the world's largest holder of foreign exchange reserves, reaching nearly one trillion dollars at the end of 2006. These reserves in turn finance the American budget deficit and Chinese investments around the world. Beijing has made huge investments and established political and economic relationships in the four corners of the planet, particularly with countries rich in energy resources and raw materials in Africa, Latin America, and the Middle East, hitherto reserved domains for Europe and the United States.

Finally, with one-sixth of the world's population, China benefits from the advantage of size, so that the access of a small percentage of its population to education and technology is enough to enable it to surpass industrialized countries in terms of human capital. It now has, for example, more than 100 million internet users, making Chinese the second language in cyberspace after English, and China the future Eldorado of electronic commerce into which the giants of the American net economy are moving with all the means at their disposal.

The second-ranking economy in the world in terms of growth rate, India is still far behind its large neighbor to the east. Turning its back on decades of the inward-looking state-run economy that followed independence, it took the first steps toward international opening and liberalization of the economy ten years after China, in 1991, in the context of negotiations for a structural adjustment loan from the IMF. Since then India has experienced annual growth on the order of 6 percent (close to 8 percent in recent years), less spectacular than China's, but nonetheless remarkable because that growth has made it possible to reduce poverty by half in twenty years, from 51 percent of the population in 1977–78 to 26 percent in 1999–2000, according to official statistics.

India's growth, like China's, depends on the development of exports and foreign investment, as well as on a huge domestic market and the dynamism of the private sector. Like the Middle Kingdom, the Indian subcontinent has an abundant and low-cost labor force, but also, unlike China, a large middle class and highly qualified English-speaking elites that are a source of competitive scientific and technological talent—the largest in the world after the United States—facilitating the integration of "shining India" into the networks of globalization. In addition to subcontracts with Western multinationals, of which it has 40 percent of the world total, India has developed cutting-edge local industries in information technology, generic pharmaceuticals (in which it is the world leader), and automobiles. The service sector, particularly computer and financial services, represents more than half of its GDP. On the international stage, it is, along with Brazil, one of the driving forces of the G20 in the framework of the WTO negotiations, where it defends its agricultural interests, and its enterprises are already widely present in the United States and Europe.

Indian growth is likely to overtake that of China by 2015, in particular because of the aging of the Chinese population and the probable slowdown of the rhythm of Chinese development in the long run. The largest democracy in the world, India would thus become the world's most populous country and its third largest economy by 2050. In 2005, when China and India together, sheltering one-third of the population of the planet and around the same percentage of the working-age population, still accounted for only 6 percent of world GDP, they contributed 40 percent of world economic growth. Before 2050 the economy of the two countries taken together is likely to become the largest in the world, twice the size of that of the United States. On an official visit to New Delhi in November 2006, Chinese President Hu Jintao argued in favor of a rapprochement between the two large Asian economic powers through trade liberalization and bilateral investments. But China and India, with growing trade and complementary economies, are also powerful competitors in high-technology industries as well as in the areas of energy supplies and international investments.

To speak of Russia as an "emerging country" after four decades of the USSR as the second global superpower may strike one as peculiar. But the Soviet Union was never a model of economic success, and, fifteen years after its implosion, Russia is still having difficulties finding a place in the world economy because of the instability of the 1990s followed by the political authoritarianism of the years since 2000. The Russian economy is now comparable in size to those of Brazil and India; forecasters envision that it will still be comparable to Brazil in 2050, but that its economy will not even be one-fourth the size of India's at that date.

Russia's economic good fortune is recent and largely tied to the soaring prices of oil and natural gas, of which it holds the largest reserves in the world. Russian GDP more than quadrupled between 1999 and 2006, and its rate of growth increased from 0 to more than 6 percent between 1995 and the first years of this century, driven by oil revenues and consumer spending. Following the opaque privatizations of the 1990s under Yeltsin, Vladimir Putin has forcefully retaken government control of the oil gas and industry and other "strategic" assets (in banking, construction, aeronautics) and placed individuals close to him at the top of major public enterprises, which now account for a solid third of the Russian economy. With the third highest market capitalization in the world, Gazprom—8 percent of Russian GDP, 300,000 employees, $ 11.7 million profit in 2005—has become a symbol of "Russia, Inc.," as much a political titan as an economic giant. At a time of scarcity provoked by Chinese and Indian demand and tensions in the Middle East, Russian energy resources have not only provided an economic windfall but have given Moscow significant political leverage over countries dependent on those resources as well, particularly its former satellites. This was manifest in the Ukrainian gas crisis of the winter of 2005, but it also affects the European Union, which purchases 26 percent of the gas it consumes from Moscow.

Following along the lines of China, Russian state capitalism aims at becoming integrated in the world economy. In 1998, the Russian Federation was admitted to the G7 (making it the G8), which it then had the honor of presiding in 2006, while being the only nondemocratic state in this putative managing board of the world economy. But the regime's authoritarian drift, the setting aside of the liberal economic reforms and of the rights established in the 1990s (as illustrated by the Yukos affair and the seizure of control of the Sakhalin-2 project from Shell and other Western multinationals), corruption, and the Kremlin's demand for reciprocity of investments in the energy sector have slowed Russia's admission to the WTO and the inflow of foreign capital while at the same time provoking Western mistrust of Russian investors.

As for Latin America's giant, Brazil, it is the smaller among the major emerging nations. The size of its economy is today comparable to that of India, but by 2050 it will be only one-fourth that country's size, while it will surpass Germany and the United Kingdom and match Japan. After a decade of alternating recession and stagnation, Brazil has returned to growth on the order of 3 or 4 percent, based on rigorous economic management resulting in a decrease in inflation, the reduction of foreign debt, and growth of exports. Its originality lies in the use it has made of the natural resources of its vast territory and of new technologies to become the largest food processing power of the developing world. Between 2000 and 2005, Brazil, now described as the "world's farm," moved from twelfth to fifth largest food exporter. Its agricultural resources have made it one of the leaders of the opposition to European and American agricultural protectionism in multilateral trade negotiations.

Subsidies and prohibitive tariffs in Western countries, however, have led Brazil to develop agricultural trade with developing countries, another original aspect of the "Brazilian model" for economic takeoff. Emerging and developing countries, particularly in Asia, already absorbed about half Brazil's agricultural exports in 2005 (compared to 20 percent fifteen years earlier), and the trend is accelerating. Here, too, the combination of raw materials and a low-cost labor force with access to research and the most modern technologies defies competition and has attracted multinational companies from the North. The rise of the emerging economies and the resulting demand has thus made it possible for Brasilia successfully to sidestep the protectionism of the North and to establish its economic takeoff on the basis of trade with other countries of the South, where it will increasingly supplant American and European exports. As an oil producer that has chosen globalization, Brazil has also distanced itself from the oil nationalism of Venezuela and Bolivia, using rather its natural resources to develop renewable energy, which has placed it at the forefront of this sector of future great importance. Ethanol already accounts for 25 percent of its energy consumption, and more than one out of three Brazilian cars runs on dual fuels (ethanol and gasoline), while biodiesel and ethanol account for an average of only 1 percent of fuel sold in a country such as France.

But its relatively modest growth rate compared to that of other large emerging countries and, most important, the weaknesses of its industrial fabric, infrastructure, educational system, and institutional apparatus will limit Brazil's rise to economic power for the foreseeable future.

GLOBALIZATION ON THE WIRE

The harshening of relations between the Arab-Muslim world and the West and the rising power of emerging countries have come to a geopolitical point of convergence in the accession of energy questions to the forefront of global concerns and international tensions. The development of a Beijing-Teheran energy axis, while the Islamic Republic is openly enriching uranium for military purposes and threatening Israel, is one of the most revealing signs of this phenomenon. A massive increase in the demand for energy linked to Asian economic growth, on the one hand, and growing concerns about the security and sustainability of oil and gas supplies, on the other, set against a background of climate change: these are the explosive elements of the new global geopolitical equation.

Indeed, since September 11, 2001, energy has more than ever been at the center of the strategy of the major producing and consuming powers, with the exception of the European Union. Rather than reducing its enormous energy consumption, the United States determined to transform Iraq, which holds the largest oil reserves in the world after Saudi Arabia, into a democratic state leaning toward the West, with the results we have seen. The fight against terrorism, as well as energy competition with Beijing and rivalry with Moscow, are more broadly behind the American military presence in the Middle East and Central Asia. For their part, Russia and other producing countries such as Iran and Venezuela have based their rise to international power on their energy resources and the political and economic leverage they provide. As for China, it has made access to energy resources and raw materials, which are essential to its pursuit of economic development, the major axis of its diplomacy and international expansion. India is likely to follow the same path. Only the EU, even though it depends on other countries for more than 55 percent of its energy consumption, is struggling to implement a common energy policy worthy of the name, while its member states, organized around one or more national champions, pursue their own strategies in disarray.

Beyond the redistribution of economic cards brought about by the rise of the emerging countries, the energy competition resulting from China's huge size has accentuated the geopolitical turn that globalization has taken. Chinese, and more broadly Asian, appetite for energy has first of all triggered harsh competition for the exploitation of new deposits between the large consuming countries—the United States, China, Europe, India, and Japan—and a continuous rise in prices of crude and other energy sources benefiting producer countries. This competition and the tensions it is causing have been reinforced by the limitations on oil and gas reserves and the strategically sensitive nature of the majority Muslim geopolitical zones in which they are located: essentially the Middle East, Central Asia, African, and Russia. Hence, as in the colonial era, access to energy resources has become the focus of complex diplomatic strategies among the great powers, a motive for territorial expansion for consuming countries, and both an economic and a political weapon in the hands of producing countries. Chinese oil companies have been investing massively and without qualms of conscience in countries endowed with oil and mineral resources, in Africa, Central Asia, and Latin America, while Putin's Russia, Ahmadinejad's Iran, the Venezuela of Chávez, and Bolivia under Morales unhesitatingly manipulate the energy weapon for political as well as economic purposes. The Kremlin's interruption of gas deliveries to Ukraine, for example, by affecting European supplies in the depths of the winter of 2005, awakened the EU to its excessive energy dependence on Russia and the attendant risks. Since then, the Kremlin's systematic resumption of control over the country's energy resources, state intervention in Russian capitalism, and Vladimir Putin's determination to impose on the West reciprocity in energy investments abroad are more reminiscent of the Soviet era than indicative of a transition to capitalism and democracy.

China's huge energy demand and that of the rest of the world, and consequent price increases, have also given rise to an enormous transfer of wealth to the producing countries, particularly to the political and entrepreneurial nomenklatura in a position to benefit from the windfall in Russia and in the oil monarchies of the Gulf. The surge in crude prices is also at the source of the economic recovery and increased power of countries such as Iran, Algeria, Venezuela, and Libya. This redistribution has in particular had the positive effect of enabling most producing countries to pay off their sovereign debt, contracted in less favorable times. It has also produced economic nationalism in Latin America and the concentration in the hands of a small elite of oligarchs and family groups in Russia, the Middle East, and Asia of financial power with no equivalent in the West. Major players in the new global capitalism, the richest investment funds on the planet are now the Abu Dhabi Investment Authority, the Saudi Arabia Investment Fund, and the Kuwait Investment Authority: the three of them together control nearly one trillion dollars in assets. A growing number of new millionaires in the global economy come from emerging countries. And China is overflowing with currency reserves to finance its international economic and diplomatic expansion. The indirect battle fought in the spring of 2006 between the Indian family group Mittal Steel, which has become the world's leading steelmaker in a few short years, and its Russian competitor Severstal, supported by the Kremlin, for control of Arcelor, heir of the European steel industry and recipient of billions of euros of governmental aid—or more recently, the unsolicited investment of the Russian state in the European aeronautics and defense concern EADS—illustrates, better than any speech, the rise to power of emerging nations and their enterprises in the world economy, but also, and most important, the changing nature of globalization and the risks associated with that change.

Since the 1980s, when this celebrated term first appeared, globalization has designated the acceleration of the process of internationalization of economies, that had in the past been essentially national, and their increasing interdependence resulting from the liberalization of markets and international trade and investment underway since the 1950s. This was an underlying trend with primarily economic content, which took the predominant form of the worldwide spread of the market economy and the opening of national economies to competition. Of American inspiration, globalization was seen primarily as a threat to European modes of economic and social organization as well as to socioeconomic arrangements in the third world. But, at the turn of the twenty-first century, globalization assumed a new face, which has substantially displaced and increased the stakes involved: it has become a geopolitical phenomenon.

The revolutionary nature of this change should not be underestimated. In conventional liberal political and economic thinking, globalization was traditionally understood as an apolitical phenomenon, indifferent to national boundaries, driven by the logic of the market alone, hence "neutral" in strategic terms and likely to foster peaceful international relations. Its detractors, on both left and right, even saw it as a threat to national identity, an unacceptable constraint weighing on democratic decision making and a corrosive force in political life, while its liberal and internationalist champions praised the peace-making and equalizing virtues of trade and the "invisible hand," building blocks of a postnational and truly "global" democracy, making the world "flat." But neither camp made any connection between globalization and geopolitics, liberalization and power strategies, trade and conflict, not to mention war and terrorism. The two principal forces for change at the dawn of the twenty-first century—the emergence of radical Islam and the spectacular rise of emerging countries—and their political and economic aftereffects have now closely bound together these two heretofore apparently antithetical sets of concerns. Globalization has indirectly transformed world geopolitics; it has increased rather than reduced international tensions, and this transformation has in turn changed the very nature of globalization.

This change, and the confusion of realms to which it has given rise, is not without consequences. On the one hand, in the West, states have largely divested themselves of capital investment in business, and their economic interventions are circumscribed by competition rules and limited by budgetary constraints. Similarly, the rules of the market, the principles of free movement of capital and freedom of investment allow foreign takeovers of industrial and financial enterprises, or even of entire sectors of a national economy, while no legal instrument or legitimate political consideration—except in the case of a few "strategic" industries whose numbers are steadily declining—allows for any opposition. On the other hand, globalization has become a geopolitical arena, in which states are often concealed behind the new capitalists of the emerging countries and do not hesitate to use economic weapons for political purposes or vice versa. Most important, it is an arena in which the parallel strengthening of nationalism and economic power confers a strategic dimension on any substantial takeover in a key industry. In other words, the depoliticization of economic movements, which has been the dogma of market-based globalization since the 1980s, will increasingly come up against the geopolitical turn of the world economic space resulting from clashes of civilizations as well as from the economic rise of continent-sized nations driven legitimately by strategic ambitions.

This growing interpenetration of economics and politics in the new globalization has rendered largely obsolete the traditional antagonism between the free market and protectionism, which made sense only within the confines of a view of the economy devoid of strategic considerations (the "strategic" sectors were considered an exception to the market rule), that is, in a world where democracy and the market economy were thought to have triumphed over nationalism, ideology, and conflict. The end of this illusion no doubt calls for a good deal of doctrinal rethinking on the part of Western political and economic authorities, particularly a redefinition of the assets that ought to be seen as affecting the security or independence of a political community, of the rules that should govern them, and a complex compromise between that strategic concern and the preservation of an open and dynamic global economy in which the United States and Europe will no longer be the sole possessors of economic and political power. The terms of such a compromise themselves depend on an assessment of the new geopolitical situation that has arisen from globalization.

One thing is certain: the geopolitical effects of globalization are no more likely than its economic and social impacts to stop its future development, barring a major conflict, or to provide better arguments for any attempt to resist it. But the geopolitical turn that globalization has taken may at least impose constraints on it, resulting from security or other concerns. This development should also lead to increased vigilance because it has coincided with a relative decline in Western democratic leadership in the world of the twenty-first century.

2

THE END OF THE
ATLANTIC ERA

Recent years have seen a good deal of debate about the "end of the West," which would supposedly result from the growing gulf between its two pillars—America and Europe—and was made evident to public opinion by the transatlantic crisis of 2002–3 over the American intervention in Iraq. According to this argument, the increasing divergence of interests, and indeed of "values," between Europe and the United States is leading to a divorce—that is, to the implosion of the West as a political reality and even as a concept of civilization. In addition to the intrinsically questionable nature of this theory,[1] the shift of the world economy toward Asia, the rise of the major emerging nations, and several other developments point in a notably different direction: not toward the implosion of the West because of a disconnection between its two components, but rather to its relative decline through a gradual loss of the dominance of world affairs that it has enjoyed since the industrial revolution of the mid nineteenth century.

Unlike the ideologically tainted notion of a transatlantic divorce, the end of the Euro-American duopoly is an objective reality, the other side of the rise of the emerging countries. It is not identical to the anticipation of the "American decline," recurrently fashionable among French intellectuals, except in a metonymic sense. The end of what I refer to here as the Atlantic era is rather the result of converging developments, among which the anticipated decline of American power is not of primary importance. Quite the contrary, we shall see that in a world that is becoming multipolar, the end of the Western duopoly is likely to have much less impact on American leadership than on the relative position of Europe.

The weakening of the West in the course of the next few decades will, first of all, result from a few fundamental macroeconomic parameters. According to the 2004 report of the Population Reference Bureau, world population is expected to increase by 45 percent to reach 9.3 billion inhabitants by the year 2050, but the bulk of this increase will take place in the developing countries. The population of industrialized countries is expected to increase by only 4 percent, with Germany, Italy, Russia, and Japan experiencing population decreases. The population of Africa is projected to increase from 13 percent of the world total in 2000 to 20 percent in 2050, with Asia remaining stable at 60 percent. Latin America, with 9 percent, is expected to surpass Europe, including Russia, reduced to 7 percent. In comparison, in 1950, the European continent accounted for one-fourth of the world's population.

Because of the economic takeoff of the developing countries, particularly in Asia, however, the intensification of the long-standing demographic marginalization of the old industrialized countries has much wider consequences than in the past. Forecasters anticipate that Chinese GDP will reach $44.453 billion in 2050 and that of India $27.803 billion, compared to $35.165 billion for the United States, and less than one-tenth that amount for a country like France. The continent with the majority of the world's population will then become also the world's strongest economic power. This historic convergence of economic power with demographic preponderance in the developing world will be reinforced by the sedentary character of Western populations in the current phase of globalization. Whereas the rise to economic power of the United States and Australia from the late nineteenth century on brought about the immigration of European populations to these

new promised lands and their consequent Europeanization, the current
rise of the emerging countries of Asia, Latin America, and Africa is occurring autonomously, with no infusion of Western populations. The
principal explanation for this lies in the demographic density of these
countries, unlike the emerging territories of the second wave of globalization, but also in the obstacles in the way of the migration of Western populations to old and deeply foreign civilizations. The West will,
therefore, have much less influence than in the past in the economic,
political, and cultural centers of tomorrow. Conversely, the migratory
pressure from countries of the East and South toward Europe and the
United States, from both extremes of the economic and social spec-
trum, will increase non-Western influence within the Western world.

BACKLASH

The decline of the Atlantic era, however, preceded the emergence of
new great economic powers in the East and South, and it represents
a much broader phenomenon than a simple redistribution of the economic cards around the world. To assess it precisely, let us begin by
identifying what the Euro-American duopoly of the last century represented, particularly since the end of the Second World War.

Although that war sealed the decline of Europe and the beginnings
of what was soon to be called the bipolar world, European reconstruction thanks to American aid, the conversion of Japan to a modern democracy, and the setbacks suffered by the Communist system quickly
restored the domination of the Western bloc over the world economy.
The United States and Europe continued to be, and remain today, the
two principal trading powers on the planet, and, at the initiative of the
United States, the industrialized countries established multilateral institutions—the OECD, the GATT, the IMF, the World Bank, the G7—that
regulated, under their aegis and largely for their own benefit, the global
economy of the second half of the twentieth century. In the political and strategic realm, the West created the United Nations, with its

claims to universality, and organized its own camp in the face of the Soviet threat through the Atlantic Alliance, the unification of Europe, and various regional organizations in Asia, Africa, and Latin America. Geopolitically, the world was divided into two blocs, East and West, and economically into three, the industrialized North dominating the developing South and competing without too much difficulty with the Communist East. Its position as leader of the "free world," victor over Nazism, and ultimate rampart against the Communist threat gave America an aura, legitimacy, an influence, and an unmatched leeway in every corner of the world. The combination of these strengths enabled the West under American leadership to define the international agenda, in both economic and political matters. Trade liberalization and the promotion of liberal democracy were the key principles.

Paradoxically, the implosion of the Soviet bloc and the end of the cold war inaugurated the difficulties of the Western camp and the decline of its global leadership. First, strategically, the disappearance of the Communist threat and the end of the bipolar East-West international system confused the geopolitical situation and loosened the bonds of solidarity of many Western countries and other allies with the United States and their political and military dependency on Washington. This was the beginning of NATO's difficulties, lacking a raison d'être since the collapse of the Soviet Union and confronted with new challenges. More broadly, Atlantic solidarity, the cornerstone of the political and economic governance of the planet during the second half of the twentieth century, began to weaken in the 1990s. Against a backdrop of illusory promises of universal peace and prosperity, it was beset by centrifugal forces, confronting a changing America that had become the only world superpower and an economically competitive European Union that was also now in search of a political identity emancipated from the American model. Media dramatization of transatlantic divergences over subjects such as the regulation of the global economy, climate change, the Israeli-Palestinian conflict, and the role of international law and multilateralism in the management of world affairs persisted after September 11, 2001, in a temporary transatlantic discrepancy in the evaluation of the terrorist threat and a much longer-lasting and deeper difference about the way to confront it, which culminated in the 2002–3 Iraqi crisis. The post–cold war period produced similar effects on relations between the United States and some of its other traditional allies in the Middle East (Turkey), Asia (South Korea), and Latin America.

The second pillar of the Atlantic order and the backbone of the revival of the European continent after the Second World War—the process of political and economic unification envisioned by Jean Monnet and Robert Schuman—was the other paradoxical victim of the end of the confrontation between East and West. Far from crowning the success of the European project, the liberation of Central and Eastern Europe from Communist oppression, German reunification, and the sudden appearance of the "Other Europe" in the construction of a European Community transformed, if not its raison d'être, at least its implicit goals and the conditions for its continued existence. Although the ultimate purpose of European unity has never been explicitly formulated, and has, even less, been a matter for consensus, the six founding members of the European Economic Community (EEC) and some of those who joined later implicitly had in mind the construction of a political and economic entity that would be able to function in the manner of a federated state. A project of this kind, however, required a strong degree of economic, political, and cultural homogeneity among its member states and a relatively limited number of participants to ensure effective governance and, even more, agreement on the essentials.

The adhesion of Great Britain, Ireland, and Denmark, followed by the expansion of the EEC from nine to twelve members compromised this twofold requirement. In 1992, when the former "people's democracies" of Central and Eastern Europe legitimately knocked at the door of the very recently established European Union, it was already much too divided over its aims and agenda, between the twelve member states and within most of them individually, to articulate any strategic vision and organize any institutional preparation for the potential doubling of its membership. Quite the contrary, throughout the 1990s enlargement helped to conceal the gradual crumbling of the European project in the post-Communist era. In the end the constantly increasing number of member states, their heterogeneity, and the absence of institutional reform and of a genuine common ambition combined their negative effects to produce the "greater Europe" of twenty-seven with declining effectiveness and still indeterminate aims and borders. Henceforth, public opinion in the founding states no longer recognized the original project, itself complex and revolutionary, and the French, as good Cartesians, were the first to proclaim that the game was over, thereby taking the risk of giving the death blow to the "political Europe" whose establishment they ritually pray for.

A consequence rather than the cause of Europe's latent existential crisis, the rejection of the EU constitutional treaty by the populations of two of the founding states marked the end of an illusion or of a hypocrisy,[2] that is, the hope to reconcile the "greater Europe" concept with the initial European Community project. Such reconciliation could only have happened had all participants agreed to establish a solidly federal structure. The no votes in France and Holland in the spring of 2005 brought an abrupt halt to the European Union's deeper integration, as well as its enlargement, and reduced its influence in the world as much as within its member states.

Thus, in the space of two years, the March 2003 American intervention in Iraq—source of the gravest tension ever experienced in transatlantic relations—and the French and Dutch rejection of the European constitutional treaty in the spring of 2005 brought to a head the twofold crisis that has simultaneously afflicted Atlantic solidarity and the construction of Europe since the fall of the Berlin Wall. Moreover, through the disagreements it provoked within the European Union about the attitude to adopt toward the American determination to intervene, the Iraqi crisis had effects that were just as harmful to European political unity as to transatlantic relations, thereby indirectly contributing to the self-inflicted defeat of the former two years later.

THE TWILIGHT OF PAX AMERICANA

Most important, the Iraqi adventure has had a devastating effect on the image and freedom of action of American power in the world, dissipating what remained of the huge worldwide prestige the United States had enjoyed during the time of the cold war. Its stock had of course already been diminished with the disappearance of the Communist threat and of Soviet and Chinese maneuvering around the world. But abuses of human rights, excesses in the fight against terrorism, and the multifaceted fiasco of the Iraq intervention have transformed the neo-anti-Americanism that arose from the United States' sole superpower status in the 1990s and was then furthered by the demonstration of its vulnerability on September 11, 2001, into a structural component of the new global geopolitics.

The Global Attitudes Survey of forty-five thousand people in forty-seven countries by the Pew Research Center confirmed in 2007, for the fifth year running since the beginning of the war in Iraq, the significant deterioration of the image of the United States in the world, even in countries traditionally considered American allies. Turkey, a NATO member and a strategic pillar of the Alliance in the Middle East, is now the country where the United States is the most unpopular, with only a 9 percent favorable opinion, confirmed by the huge success of the violently anti-American film *Valley of the Wolves Iraq*. In Europe only 23 percent of the Spanish public had a positive opinion of the United States in 2006, compared to 41 percent in 2005. In a country that was also hit hard by Islamist terrorism in 2004, 76 percent of those surveyed were opposed to the "war against terror" as conceived in Washington. Guantanamo and Abu Ghraib are familiar names to nine out of ten people in Europe and Japan, more than in the United States itself. The only countries where a majority still exists in favor of the American view of the war against terrorism are Russia and India, both threatened by Islamism; but even there anti-Americanism has markedly increased. In ten of the fifteen countries surveyed in 2006, a majority of the public believed the world is more dangerous because of the Iraqi conflict. This was notably the opinion of 60 percent of the British, whose troops have been engaged alongside the Americans. This opinion is now widely shared by the American public itself, contrary to the constant argument of the Bush administration to justify the intervention in Iraq. Even worse, according to a Louis Harris survey published by the Financial Times in June 2006, 36 percent of Europeans (in Great Britain, Germany, France, Italy, and Spain) now see the United States as the principal threat to world stability, ahead of Iran (30 percent) and China (18 percent).

Behind these startling figures, two alarming transformations in the relations of the United States with the rest of the world are taking shape. The first, which we have already mentioned, is the prospect of a continuing conflict between America (and through it the whole of the Western community) and the Arab-Muslim world, no longer centered only on the Israeli-Palestinian conflict but broadened to include the dispute over the intervention in Iraq, the confrontation with Iran, the all-out war against Islamist terrorism, and cultural and religious issues. This was not always the case, as the United States was long the subject of real fascination within the Arab world and exerted considerable influence because of its economic and military power and its ability to put pressure on Israel. The second area of concern is the change in Washington's relations with its postwar European and Asian allies, in whose eyes the combination of arrogance, unilateralism, and vulnerability that has characterized America after September 11 now appears to be an additional destabilizing factor in a dangerous world. The time when the United States was looked on as leader, guarantor, or mediator of local or regional conflicts seems a distant memory. The new tension between Islam and the West is thus largely attributed to American foreign policy by European, Arab, and Asian public opinion, with direct consequences for popular feeling about the United States and, indirectly, for the range of options open to allied and moderate governments with respect to Atlantic solidarity. European acceptance of decisive leadership by the United States in international affairs has thus fallen sharply in the last three years. If we add the increasing economic and ideological rivalry between America and Europe, as well as other major Asian and Latin American allies of Washington, the loss of influence and prestige—the vaunted "soft power"—of the United States appears to have been substantial.

Bogged down in Iraq with a force of over 160,000 following the 2007 "surge" and beset by widespread hostility in the Arab-Muslim world, George W. Bush's America has had limited military, diplomatic, and political freedom of movement to deal with nuclear provocation from North Korea and Iran, to restore order in the Middle East and Afghanistan, or to counter the revived power of its traditional rivals, Moscow and Beijing. Since late 2004 the arrogant unilateralism of the first Bush administration and the recourse to "coalitions of the willing" have fortunately given way to consultation with the Europeans and calls on other great powers (the EU, Russia, China) to negotiate with Tehran and Pyongyang as well as on the UN to impose sanctions, much to the dismay of residual neoconservatives. But the damage has been done, and the weakening of America, a boon to its many adversaries, is a handicap for peace.

THE CRISIS OF MULTILATERALISM

The vicissitudes of the European project, the most fully developed experiment in regional integration and governance, are emblematic of a larger phenomenon: the slow drift of the multilateral institutional system devised by the United States following the Second World War in the face of global developments and the emergence of new actors. These institutions were politically and intellectually dominated for half a century by the United States and the other industrialized countries, and some of them, such as the G7 and the Trilateral Commission, were their exclusive preserve. From the outset, the UN alone had granted a right of veto to the Soviet Union and subsequently China as permanent members of the Security Council, which resulted in a relative marginalization of that institution, a symbol of multilateralism, in the management of major regional conflicts, aggravated by third world domination of the General Assembly and, lately, by unilateral actions by the United States.

The twin Bretton Woods institutions—the International Monetary Fund and the World Bank—long embodied the domination of industrialized countries over developing ones through the dogmatic imposition of liberal economic reforms in inappropriate social and economic circumstances. But the social devastation and growing unpopularity of "structural adjustment programs," and other austerity cures imposed on poor countries by the IMF, as well as the Asian, Latin American, and Russian financial crises of the late 1990s gradually weakened both bodies. In recent years, thanks to the oil bonanza, the restoration of public finances in many emerging countries has significantly reduced their need for financing from the IMF and the World Bank, calling into question the traditional mission of those institutions. The failure of the "Washington consensus" in support of policies fostering austerity, liberalization, and privatization in many poor countries of Africa and Latin America has also driven the World Bank toward greater modesty. In the face of the sui generis takeoff of China and India, new global creditors, and the stagnation of many poor client states of the two Washington institutions, the developing world will soon have no need to receive instructions in economic policy from the West.

The evolution of the World Trade Organization (WTO)—now the most important multilateral institution in the economic field—provides the clearest illustration of the contemporary crisis of multilateralism. The WTO was established in 1995 to provide a more structured and universal framework than GATT—a simple trade agreement established in 1948—for the liberalization and regulation of world trade. However, whereas GATT had succeeded from the 1960s through 1994 in completing several rounds of world trade liberalization, which provided the foundation for growth, globalization, and the takeoff of emerging countries, the WTO has experienced a series of failures. As a symbol of "free market globalization," even though it in fact guarantees the regulation of globalization through a system of negotiated and enforceable multilateral norms, it became the preferred target of antiglobalization movements and the radical left in nations of both North and South, which lay behind the demonstrations and the collapse of the 1999 Seattle summit. A few weeks after the shock of September 11, 2001, rightly understood as a threat to the pursuit of globalization, the WTO attempted to revive multilateral trade negotiations in Doha (Qatar), within the framework of a "development round" that intended to foster more equitable trade, enabling the least advanced countries to participate in the world economy. One of the principal objectives of the Doha round was to lower barriers to the entry of agricultural products from the developing world into the American and European markets. But negotiations suffered another setback at the Cancun conference, which marked the entry onstage of the major emerging countries united in the G20 under the determined leadership of Brazil and India, rising agricultural powers. The developing world is intent on pursuing the reduction of American and European subsidies and customs duties hindering exports of the major countries of the South to the North as well as to other developing countries. In return, the United States and the European Union are seeking the liberalization of markets for manufactured products and services in the emerging countries. After three further years of effort, negotiations were suspended in July 2006: competition between Europe and the United States, powerful agricultural lobbies on both sides of the Atlantic, and the European agreement protecting the EU Common Agricultural Policy until 2013 made sufficient concessions on the part of the various stakeholders impossible. After almost ten years of frustrating negotiations, the failure of the Doha round has damaged the credibility of the WTO and left the field open to a proliferation of bilateral or regional liberalization agreements that now govern 40 percent of world trade, with a lack of transparency that is unfavorable to the poorest countries and fosters trade wars among the richest.

While the entry of the G20 as an organized force into the complex dynamics of multilateral trade negotiations was of course an added complicating factor, the WTO's difficulties are primarily attributable to the rule of consensus (in principle, unanimity) prevailing among its

150 member states. Multilateralism has here come up against its major contradiction and limit. Its success has attracted a growing number of countries, which its universal principles also compel it to accept. But in the absence of federalist decision-making rules based on qualified majorities, the effect of numbers and the heterogeneity resulting from the continuing openness of multilateral institutions to new members has gradually reduced their effectiveness to the point of paralysis and marginalization. They even completely lose their purpose when laxity and opportunism win out over rigorous criteria for admission. The UN Human Rights Commission, for example, did not survive its Libyan presidency, and the Council of Europe, guardian of human rights, saw its credibility threatened when it admitted Russia. Even in the absence of such missteps, the effectiveness and legitimacy of multilateral institutions have had a good deal of difficulty withstanding the weakening of the Atlantic duopoly. The G7, a sort of managing board of the major industrialized democracies when it was created in 1975, has gradually been changed into a media "circus" of no great consequence, challenged by antiglobalization summits, and now including Russia, which presided over its July 2006 meeting. In the strategic field the nuclear nonproliferation treaty (NPT), a pillar of collective security since 1968, has now been overtly flouted by North Korea and more subtly by Iran.

This disintegration has only aggravated another Achilles' heel of multilateralism: the Washington's traditional ambivalence toward it. A power jealous of its sovereignty, the United States invented the multilateral system to organize the world rather than to subject itself to the system's constraints. The post–cold war period, characterized by the triumph of the American model and the ineffectiveness and increasing anti-Americanism of certain multilateral entities, has only strengthened a historical attitude that has oscillated between the benevolent opportunism of the Clinton era and the destructive contempt of the neoconservatives of the first Bush administration.

As with the construction of Europe, this generalized drift of multilateralism has played into the hands of nationalism, encouraging each country to defend its own interests in the huge global and regional donnybrooks that multilateral meetings have become, or bilateral negotiations in the sidelines, for want of the collective solidarity that once made the strength of multilateralism. Harmful to the governance of the planet at a time when globalization and multipolarity cry out more than ever for rules, the crisis of multilateralism has also produced specific perverse effects in the old industrialized countries by intensifying the feeling of Western societies that they have lost control over their own fate.

THE DEMOCRATIC RECESSION

In addition to the loss of international influence that is its principal manifestation, another aspect of the weakening of the Atlantic duopoly is indeed the crisis of leadership and political legitimacy that is rife within most Western democracies. This has taken diverse forms, often cumulative: weak support for parties and governments in power, division of the electorate creating very narrow majorities to govern, weak international stature of national political leaders, triumph of popular opinion over political vision and courage, the rise of populism and extremism.

The causes of this situation are many, but they all have as a backdrop the growing gap between a world with ever more complex globalized economic and political determinants that are difficult to master (markets, multilateral negotiations, unilateral decisions with international effects) and democratic societies confined within the ever narrower and increasingly irrelevant framework of the nation-state   that are nonetheless increasingly demanding in terms of participation and control. This gap has set in opposition to one another national democratic processes and the various institutional frameworks of globalization (the EU, the WTO . . .), notably in European societies particularly exposed by their conservatism and rigidity to the challenges of global competition. In this context the dominance of public opinion democracy has led to an increasingly marked provincialism of the political classes and of national debates. This has in turn widened the initial gap between national democracies and global governance, depriving the latter of the leadership capacity demonstrated by American and European political elites in the course of the postwar decades and stripping the Atlantic duopoly of some of its past influence. The fight against terrorism and the promotion of democracy are the only areas in which the Bush administration has exercised some degree of international leadership, quickly undermined by the war in Iraq, the scandals of Abu Ghraib and Guantanamo, and the upsurge of anti-Americanism in the world. In Europe Tony Blair and Jacques Chirac were able for a time to promote matters of worldwide concern such as development, Africa, climate change, and, in the case of Blair, the construction of European unity itself, before they were reduced to silence by their domestic political setback. As for the promotion of democracy, in the eyes of Western public opinion, it has increasingly taken on the negative contours of the Iraqi civil war, in the United States, and the admittance of Turkey to the EU, in Europe.

Conversely, in the face of public sensitivity to the social and economic effects of globalization, European political leaders, and to a lesser extent their American counterparts, have not had the courage to address head-on the challenges posed to industrialized societies by the economic, political, and cultural rise of the major emerging countries, and the unavoidable necessity of adapting to this situation. Here, too, Western democracies have suffered from a twofold handicap in comparison to countries with a long authoritarian tradition, such as China and Russia, in which the political leadership finds it all the easier to mobilize the masses around direct governmental action because globalization is synonymous with both prosperity and recovered national pride and even with a relative liberalization.

This shrinking of the field of vision of democratic societies has rather naturally been accompanied by a symmetrical decline in the global influence of the political and economic model that came out of the Enlightenment and the industrial revolution. Democracy and liberal reformism, in Western Europe's backyard, have regressed in the new EU member states, giving way to nationalism and populism encouraged by the disappointing recess of European unification. The internal crisis of Western democracies, the failures of the war against terrorism, the setbacks to the American policy of promoting democracy in the Middle East, and most important the growing and sometimes triumphalist affirmation of national, religious, and cultural identities everywhere in the world have combined their effects to legitimate a global and increasingly open challenge to the universal character of democratic values, contradicting the utopian and "politically correct" visions of the post–cold war period. This rejection is, of course, most notable in the Iran of the mullahs and in radical Islamist circles, but it has spread widely through the Arab-Muslim world on the basis of religious and ideological criteria and has even reached the heart of European societies, where it poses a serious challenge to secularism. The rejection of the Western conception of democracy, human rights, and the market economy has also been asserted with increasing clarity by Russia under Putin, China, the Venezuela of Chávez, and other emerging countries, in the name of cultural diversity, differences in the level of development, or a mere opportunistic political assertion of sovereignty and the national interest in opposition to the dominant Western model. The success of the Chinese, Russian, or Turkish economic model, combining a market economy with state control, opening to the world with economic nationalism, formal democracy with authoritarianism, and capitalism with Islam, provides a powerful underpinning for an ideological challenge to the universality, not to mention the superiority, of the political and economic model and the values of the West. In Africa, the Middle East, Latin America, and Asia, the political, economic, and cultural influence of Europe and the United States has declined as a consequence of nationalism, anti-Americanism, third worldism, and the growing strength of China and other emerging countries. In the essential area of information the Western monopoly of worldwide means of communication has been challenged by the decentralizing effect of the Internet and the entry of international broadcasters like Al Jazeera into the English-language global media market. But there is often a very thin line between a healthy competition of viewpoints, on the one hand, and, on the other, a relativist challenge to liberal demo-

cratic values and the promotion of new forms of totalitarianism arising
in the East, a region of the planet toward which the center of gravity of
the world economy is simultaneously shifting.

BRAIN POWER MOVES EAST

The most significant aspect of the relative decline of the West in coming
decades will, of course, be the economic rise of Asia and other emerging countries, which has already made its presence felt in the increasing competition of the labor force of those countries in manufacturing
and some service industries with low added value. This has led to an
international division of labor marked by outsourcing, deindustrializa-
tion, and massive job losses in the United States and Europe as well as
in some developing countries, such as Romania and Tunisia, that have
been unable to weather Asian competition. China has thus become the
"world's workshop," India the preferred location for the outsourcing
of computer services, and South Korea a global factory for electronic equipment. While it has weakened social structures and deepened
trade deficits in industrialized countries, this first stage in the rise to
power of emerging countries has at least had a less visible counterpart
in lower prices for a large number of goods and services for Western
businesses and consumers. The next stage, which is now in progress,
is of much more significant macroeconomic and strategic dimension.
Thanks to its massive trade surpluses and a national savings rate of 45
percent, China has for several years been financing huge American budget deficits. Its equally gigantic raw material and energy needs have
consistently kept world prices at a high level, to the detriment of the
United States and Europe and to the benefit of major producing countries such as Russia. The resulting financial power, variously derived
from economic growth, trade surpluses, oil earnings, and national savings, has made possible the establishment of "national champions" in
the principal economic sectors, often public or under state control, that
are destined to become major players in the new globalized economy.

In 2004 the alliance of the French electronics group Thompson with TCL (China) for the production of television sets and the purchase of the PC business of IBM by Lenovo symbolized the entry of the new "New World" into industries that not so long ago had been emblems of advanced Western technology. Since then the West has seen the aborted acquisition of the California oil company Unocal by the Chinese oil company CNOOC and, most important, the victorious offensive of the Indian family-owned business Mittal, now the second largest steelmaker in the world, for control of Arcelor, the outcome of twenty years of costly restructuring of the European steel industry, whose only alternative would have been to place its fate in the hands of its Russian partner Severstal, with Moscow's blessing. Western leaders and public opinions have also become familiar with Gazprom and Rosneft, results of the resumption of political control over the Russian gas and oil industries intended to maximize the economic and political leverage conferred on the Kremlin by the country's energy resources. They have gradually become acquainted with the names of the future multinationals from the emerging world—Huawey (China, television sets), SAIC (China, automobiles), Infosys (India, information technology), Ranbaxy (India, pharmaceuticals), Hyundai (South Korea, electronics), Petrobras (Brazil, energy), and many others—setting out to take over Western companies.

But the third stage in the rise to power of the emerging economies—the one that will be the most decisive for the redistribution of global economic hierarchies—still lies in the future. Until now, despite increasing competition from the developing world in more and more sophisticated manufactured products as well as in agriculture, the United States and Europe have been able to find reassurance in claiming to maintain their leadership in businesses involving advanced technology and high value-added intellectual content, the keys to scientific progress, technological innovation, and future growth. This hope now appears increasingly illusory.

The new Asian economic powers are already no longer satisfied with a role as subcontractors in industries with significant technological content, such as electronics and computers, and they are getting ready to compete with their Western suppliers and partners by requiring from them technology transfers in aeronautics, nuclear energy, and other key industries: the power they hold because of the size of their markets and the intensity of international competition have made this easy for them, as the French nuclear group Areva recently learned to its detriment.

In the longer term, Western scientific and technological leadership, particularly that of the United States, is under threat from Asian ambitions and resources in research and development, higher education, and training. In their historic effort to catch up with the industrialized West, China, India, and other emerging countries on a smaller scale, have fully grasped that economic competition in the twenty-first century will operate principally in the realm of knowledge and the intangible economy, that is, investment in educational systems, scientific and technical training, and research and development. Whereas the number of American scientists and engineers has continued to decline, and the gap separating Europe from the United States in the area has grown even greater, in less than twenty-five years China has become a global scientific and technological power, a goal that has been a constant priority of the government since the reforms of 1978. It is now second only to the United States in R&D expenditure, having surpassed Japan, with the aim of soon reaching 2.5 percent of GDP.[3] Still weak in fundamental research, this investment is concentrated on technological innovation, made necessary as much by economic development itself as by its ecological consequences and China's lack of natural resources in relation to the size of its population. Thanks to the leverage provided by its domestic market, the kingdom of piracy and counterfeiting is now developing an active strategy for the development of local industrial property with the encouragement of the WTO. Size also impacts the flow of university students undertaking scientific studies in the university, which has increased in a generation from 1.4 to 20 percent of the relevant population, amounting to a number of students equivalent to those in Europe and the United States combined. After evaluating institutions of higher education and research around the world, China is investing billions of dollars in the creation of world-class universities able to rival major American institutions in the global competition for brain power.

India has also made human capital the major axis of its development, and its growth in information technology and biotechnology has been so rapid that the five hundred thousand engineers that graduate each year from its universities and institutes of technology are no longer enough to meet national and international demand. The operation of the market and in China's case a deliberate policy of rewarding researchers according to results have gradually brought local earnings closer to Western levels, accelerating the return home of graduates who had been expatriates in the United States and even inciting Western emigration to the new technological paradises of Asia.

The foreseeable end of the monopoly of the old industrialized countries over advanced scientific and technical training and the aging of the Western population are fostering another revolutionary phenomenon: the globalization of the R&D activities of multinational companies, that is, its massive outsourcing to emerging countries, with China and India once again in the front rank. According to the United Nations Commission for Trade and Development (UNCTAD), before 2010 the Middle Kingdom may become the principal location for research activities of multinational companies, representing hundreds of billions of dollars, ahead of the United States and India. The combination of domestic endeavors and foreign contributions is thus helping to make Chindia the future center of global technological innovation of the twenty-first century. The National Bureau of Economic Research has confirmed it: the globalization of the scientific and technological workforce and increasing competition from emerging countries in this market will eventually threaten American scientific and technological leadership and the position of American industry in advanced technology sectors.[4]

AN ASYMMETRICAL DECLINE

In the economic sphere the weakening of the Atlantic duopoly thus first translates into a decline of the domination the United States exercised over the process of globalization in the second half of the twentieth century. In addition to its scientific and technological dimension, this "de-Americanization" of globalization has many characteristics: a reduction of the American share of global exports from 25 percent in the postwar period to 9 percent; the fading out of worldwide symbols of American industrial leadership (the near bankruptcy of General Motors, the shrinkage of IBM, Coca-Cola's difficulties); the transfer of the electronics industry to Asia; the continuing difficulty in concluding a new round of world trade liberalization since the 1990s; the decreased drawing power of overregulated American financial markets faced with rising competition from European and Asian exchanges; the erosion of American "cultural imperialism" linked to the wider decline in the "soft power" of the United States around the world, to cultural diversity and to the emergence of cultural industries with international ambitions, such as the Bollywood phenomenon in India, which is now more popular in Africa than American film. Some would add the growing dependency of the American economy on the rest of the world, particularly on China, for its financing and consumption, which illustrates deeper integration of the American superpower into the global economy rather than the latter's "de-Americanization." In contrast, the European Union, the largest trading power in the world, with its own international currency and an organized market of 490 million consumers, is in the view of some on an ascending path, participating along with Asia in a slowly developing challenge to American leadership.

Yet, regardless of what the professional prophets of American decline maintain, this analysis is in fact deceptive. While it is natural that the changes underway seem to be occurring principally to the detriment of the dominant superpower, this in no way means that the United States is badly positioned to confront the new world order, or that Europe is in a better position. Since the early 1990s up to the financial crisis of 2007, in periods of rapid expansion and of slowdown, the American economy has enjoyed a growth rate twice that of the European Union. Thanks to consumer spending, it has survived relatively intact the bursting of the Internet bubble, the 2001 recession, the September 11 attacks, military intervention in Afghanistan and Iraq, and the surge in oil prices. American companies are still dominant among the highest market capitalization figures in the world, with Microsoft, Wal-Mart, and Pfizer replacing IBM, General Motors, and Coca-Cola. Indeed, unlike Europe, the United States possesses a number of assets that will enable it to continue to play in the big leagues in the twenty-first century.

Like the new great economic powers, the United States is first of all a continental nation, that is, it has a territory, a population, and a market of continental size, while at the same time enjoying the unity, social bonds, identity, and capacity for political engagement characteristic of nations. America is, of course, a pluralist and decentralized democracy and not a state ruled by an authoritarian and centralized government, but the attendant freedom is generally viewed in the West as an asset, not a handicap. The European Union, for its part, is a continental area and a large market, but it will never be a nation-state, and its political identity is diluting as it expands.

Demography also connects the United States with the new economic powers. Thanks to significant numbers of immigrants, coming in particular from Asia, and to a high fertility rate (2.1, i.e., the critical population replacement rate, in 2006), especially in the Hispanic population, the United States' population could approach 500 million in 2050, compared to 281 million in 2000, and 300 million in 2006. Its median age would remain stable at around 34, while the median in Europe is estimated to move from 37.7 to 52.7, with those over 65 accounting for some 60 percent of the population. The United States would thus be the only large industrialized country to maintain a rate of demographic growth close to those of the principal emerging nations of the South, and it will remain the third most populous nation on the planet, after India and China, and ahead of Indonesia, Pakistan, and Brazil. Taking into account the importance of human capital in future economic growth, and the economic, financial, and social handicaps associated with aging and declining populations, this represents a major resource for the once New World.

The United States' continuing capacity to absorb immigrants is in part the result of two specific characteristics that in the long term probably represent its greatest assets in the twenty-first-century world: the universality of the English language and America's status as the planet's university at a time when the competitive standing of its higher education system has become a major strategic advantage for a nation. The excellence of major American universities and research institutions and their capacity for absorption and integration have justifiably attracted the best students in the world, who go there to complete their education and then, in many cases, put their talents at the service of the American economy for a certain period of time. Aside from the demographic aspect, this unique status as global university has given the United States several other advantages: a constant and difficult-to-quantify flow of brain power from the academic world into the productive economy, a form of globalization of the vital forces of American society, already imbued with multiculturalism from the country's beginnings, a capacity to define global standards for teaching, research, and professional practices and, furthermore, to influence the intellectual agenda and ways of thinking of global elites from one end of the planet to the other. This range of special attributes, which supplement the well-known dynamism of American society and compensate for the declining leadership of the United States in the political and cultural realms, will keep Uncle Sam at the heart of tomorrow's global economy. Even after China has surpassed it, the American economy will thus maintain the second rank in the world, far ahead of Japan and India.

Finally, unlike Europe, the United States has two other major assets that will preserve its preeminence in the twenty-first-century world: a military power with no equivalent in the world that it is determined to maintain, as evidenced by the staggering increase in the defense budget since September 11, 2001, and a mastery of innovation (as distinct from a mere research and development capability) in information technology, communications, and biotechnology, the three industries that will shape our future, which Asia is unlikely to match anytime soon.

The combination of these resources will enable the United States to remain the greatest world power or, at the very least, the principal interlocutor for a China whose rise will mark the twenty-first century. The situation of Europe is entirely different: it will have a good deal of difficulty in asserting itself in a multipolar world that may well be dominated by a Sino-American duopoly.

3

THE GEOPOLITICS OF GLOBALIZATION

What do the tidal waves observable at the threshold of the twenty-first century—the rise of radical Islam around the world, the emergence of new economic powers with global stature, the relative weakening of the West—hold in store for us over the next few decades? By what organizing principle is the new course of international relations governed? What will the geopolitics of the twenty-first century look like? In order to approach these questions, revisiting prevalent anticipations at the time of the fall of the Berlin Wall may be a useful point of departure.

TWENTY-FIRST-CENTURY SCHIZOID WORLD

The opening of the post–cold war period at the turn of the 1990s witnessed an opposition between two equally celebrated and controversial paradigms of the development of international relations. The first was Francis Fukuyama's thesis of the "end of history," emblematic of the spirit of the age, according to which the defeat of Communism marked the failure of the last ideology competing against liberal democracy and capitalism, which were thenceforth destined to bestow their benefits on the entire planet.[1] The spread of the market economy, even to formerly Communist countries, the prospect of those countries and even of Russia itself joining NATO, and utopian propositions about the "peace dividend" and the new international order briefly seemed to validate this optimistic vision, until history gradually reappeared on stage, from the Rwandan genocide of 1994 to the antiglobalist demonstrations in Seattle and Genoa a few years later, from ethnic cleansing in the Balkans to the tragedy of September 11, 2001, not to mention the Tienanmen massacre as early as the spring of 1989.

In contrast, the paradigm of the "clash of civilizations" sketched by Samuel Huntington put the emphasis on the substitution of ethnic, cultural, and religious rivalries for the ideological confrontation over socioeconomic systems that had dominated the cold war.[2] More out of phase than Fukuyama's with the euphoric atmosphere of the early 1990s, Huntington's argument was considered excessively pessimistic and then accused of embodying the danger of self-fulfilling prophecies as the atrocities of ethnic wars and the emergence of the antagonism between Islam and the West seemed to substantiate it.

Both dismissed, the first for its lack of realism, the second for its subversive character, the theses of the end of history and of the clash of civilizations nonetheless continue to inform, in their very contrast, contemporary visions of the evolution of the international system. Fukuyama's thesis, revised and corrected to take into account the various forms of resistance provoked by the monopolistic rule of the market and democracy, inspired American neoconservative thinking, the "transformational" diplomacy of the second Bush administration in favor of the democratization of the Middle East and its integration into the world economy, but also the European Union's enlargement policy and, more generally, the renewed faith in trade, globalization, technology, multilateralism, and "global governance" as forces for peace and development, in other words, the essential part of Western diplomacy with respect to the rest of the world. Not so bad for a discredited argument . . . As for Huntington, persona non grata in the realm of aspirations, he has triumphed in the real world: once the illusions of the post–cold war period dissipated, the world of the first decade of the new century, marked by tensions between Islam and the West, the historical reemergence of non-Western great powers, and the ethnic and nationalistic fragmentation of the planet, bears a striking resemblance to the common understanding of the "clash of civilizations."

The point of convergence between Fukuyama and Huntington— since there is no reason to choose between them—is, of course, globalization, because the confrontation between East and West as the organizing principle of the postwar world in fact was succeeded by nothing other than globalization itself. From it has flowed the global redistribution of economic and hence political power, in favor of the emerging countries. To it can also be attributed, at least partially, the renewed rise of anti-Americanism in the world, the radicalization of Islam, and its confrontation with the West. In the realm of geopolitics, globalization has produced three contradictory effects: economic and cultural integration and homogenization reducing conflict—the notion that "the world is flat," derived from traditional liberal ideas; in the opposite direction, resistance and radicalization based on ethnic or national identity against this homogenizing movement of the dominant culture and economy, a source of fragmentation and conflict; and, finally, a reorganization of the existing economic hierarchy, also the source of possible destabilization and conflict. The combination of these competing forces has engendered a dualistic world simultaneously on the path of integration and that of fragmentation, sometimes described as a multipolar world. That concept does make it possible to account for the complexity of the geopolitical effects of globalization and the duality to which it has given rise, that is, the dissemination of power among a multiplicity of centers, which may in varying degrees be homogeneous or in conflict, all within a single "globalized" and irreducibly interdependent universe. However, while it may describe the configuration of the world into which we are entering, the concept of multipolarity has no normative or "strategic" virtue and can in no way constitute an organizing principle for the new international system:

a multipolar world may even be a synonym for chaos. International relations theorists are far from unanimous on the respective advantages of a multipolar, bipolar, or unipolar system from the point of view of world peace and stability. There is no question that the two world wars took place in a multipolar context, whereas the bipolar world of the cold war and the post–cold war unipolar world avoided the internationalization of conflicts and guaranteed a certain stability.

The geopolitics of the early twenty-first century are in fact the chaotic result of conflicting forces: on one side, increasing fragmentation and conflict around national, territorial, ethnic, religious, or cultural dividing lines, on the other, as a sort of countermedicine, diversely successful diplomatic efforts to promote the adhesion of "deviant" states to the multilateral system and to globalization along with the benefits of democracy. These diplomatic efforts are primarily those of the West, Europe and the United States alike, even though for various reasons American rhetoric is more fully developed in this area than that of the EU. But the language of integration into the international system is, of course, also adopted by the states to which it is addressed—for two reasons. This integration first of all corresponds to their enlightened self-interest in terms of power; but the commitment to accept integration also allows them to gain time and distract the West's attention from the buildup of economic and/or military power over which the "international community" will soon have no control. This is clearly the strategy adopted by Iran in seeking to follow in North Korea's footsteps by presenting the world with the fait accompli of military nuclear capability. And, in the economic realm, this is China's strategy to fulfill the ambitions that might make it, by mid-century, the primary world power.

Diplomacy has, therefore, assumed the appearance of a race against the clock and a wager on the future or of a fools' game, depending on one's point of view. For optimists, the essential thing is to draw in as quickly as possible states that may pose threats to the international system, on the assumption that they would thereafter have no further interest in using their power for aggressive purposes. Using the carrot and the stick, and based on the idea that power creates obligations, this traditional policy of "engagement" is aimed at linking support and official recognition of the rising power of the states concerned to their adoption of responsible behavior toward the international community in economic, diplomatic, military, and environmental matters. It led the Western democracies to admit post-Communist Russia to the Council of Europe in 1996 and the G8 in 1998, China to the WTO in 2001, and to negotiate with North Korea and Iran on the path to nuclear power. This policy of engaging and encouraging the assumption of international responsibility remains the keystone of Western diplomacy toward any deviant state as long as it claims to belong to the international community and plays the game to however slight an extent.

For pessimists, on the other hand, real or apparent integration into the international system is, for the states concerned, only an instrument at the service of a strategy of power: time is thus necessarily running against the West, in the very short term in the case of Iran's acquisition of nuclear capability, in the much longer term with regard to China's rise to superpower status. This skepticism is based on the frequent failure of policies of accommodation in the absence of a favorable balance of power: wasn't it American superiority that in the end brought about the collapse of the Soviet Union and Western firmness that forced Qaddafi's Libya to give up terrorism? Other lessons drawn from the recent past point in the same direction. The presumed democratic virtues of economic development are belied by the Chinese or Russian models, combining capitalism with posttotalitarianism. Similarly, the rise of radical Islamist parties in the Arab world and the setbacks of the United States in Iraq have compromised faith in the pacifying effects of democratization and discredited the American dream of a "new Middle East." Democracy can, of course, not be reduced to the holding of free elections, nor capitalism to a growth rate, even a double digit one. But the belief in the automatic nature of the beneficial side effects of economic development and democratization has taken a serious blow.

THE RETURN OF EMPIRES

Against this backdrop, while being careful to avoid the parallel pitfalls of excessive naïveté and paranoia, how are we to read the new international system? Let us first observe that the fog obscuring geopolitical landmarks that characterized the post–cold war decade has now dissipated. The Russian-American "strategic partnership" of the Yeltsin period has fizzled and been replaced by the return of a more conflict-laden relationship, sometimes reminiscent of the cold war. The restoration of state control over the Russian economy, Vladimir Putin's growing authoritarianism, and the Kremlin's aggressive foreign energy policy have trumped the convergence of interest between Washington and Moscow in the fight against Islamist terrorism. Relations between Russia and the European Union are also tense, for the same reasons, and they are aggravated by geographical proximity, energy interdependence, and Europe's attractive force for the former Soviet republics located on its eastern borders. Similarly, Chinese-American relations have seen the accumulation of areas of tension, from Beijing's trade and monetary policies to its appetite for energy and mining resources, from struggles for influence in East Asia to the repercussions of China's economic and diplomatic activism in Africa and the Middle East. The difficulties the West has faced in securing Russian and Chinese adherence to sanctions resolutions against Iran and North Korea in the Security Council have also recalled the finest hours of the confrontation between East and West.

While the old bipolar organization of the world is definitively over and done with, such reminiscences are not completely lacking in relevance. Putin's Russia has openly displayed its ambition to restore the prestige and power of the former Soviet Union (and of Tsarist Russia before it), both on the perimeter and within the sphere of influence of the USSR and more broadly on the international stage. This ambition has necessarily led to hostile relations with the enemy of the past, which is now the world's only superpower, and, to a lesser extent, with the European Union, a more attractive competitor than the Kremlin in the eyes of Ukraine, Belarus, Georgia, and other states that Moscow still considers its "near abroad." As for China, it is still a Communist republic and a rival power for the United States and Japan in East Asia, is rapidly becoming their principal economic competitor in globalization, and is preparing to share world strategic leadership with the United States within a few decades. It is as though the two centers of the Communist world of yesterday had traded in their failing economic systems for globalized capitalism in order to resume on a stronger footing the competition with their great historic rival.

Beyond this return to a form of latent confrontation between the principal protagonists of the cold war, the geopolitics of the early twenty-first century has little in common with the period from 1950 to 1989. After the unipolar parenthesis of the 1990s, dominated by a triumphant America, we have witnessed the advent of a multipolar world, marked by the emergence of new economic and political powers in Asia and Latin America, not to mention the European Union itself. Fortunately, most of these new power centers pose no foreseeable threat to international security or to the West. States such as India—with which the United States has recently signed a revolutionary cooperation agreement in civilian nuclear energy—but also South Korea, Brazil, Mexico, and South Africa—because of their democratic character, their history, and their geographical location—clearly belong to this category, even though their political and economic weight on the international stage will continue to grow, as already evidenced by the influence of the G20 in the WTO and the candidacies of several of them for a permanent seat on the UN Security Council. Efforts by Brazil, India, and South Africa to unify and embody a democratic and globalist "Southern pole" on the international stage have, on the contrary, opened a positive alternative path in opposition to the aggressive anti-American nationalism of Venezuela president Hugo Chávez and his extremist allies. On the other hand, the reemergence of Iran, Russia, and, most important, China as international powers clearly carries with it a strategic dimension that is likely to determine the geopolitics of the twenty-first century.

In contrast with the states mentioned earlier, these three major nations are old empires with illustrious histories, inspired by a feeling of exceptional status and a strong national ambition, completely mobilized toward the reconquest of their status as international powers with the support of their populations. They are also nations with authoritarian traditions, with totalitarian pasts, alien to Western democratic and liberal culture, indeed in explicit breach with that culture, and engaged, by their history and their will to power, in a structurally hostile relationship with the West, embodied by the United States. All three have sought to clothe their exacerbated nationalism in an ideological or religious mantle to establish their international influence. At the same time, all three have a feeling of vulnerability with respect to their geographical surroundings and to American power, which fosters their aggressiveness. These common characteristics have given the rise of Iran, Russia, and China a similar strategic dimension, but one that is expressed very differently through each of them.

THE IRANIAN THREAT

Iran has for several years been at the center of the international community's concerns because of its determination, unacknowledged but obvious, to acquire military nuclear capacity, aggravated by the anti-Western, anti-Israeli, and anti-Semitic radicalism of the government elected in 2005. The Iranian nuclear program, conducted clandestinely since 1987 in violation of the nuclear nonproliferation treaty, has been the subject of difficult negotiations with the international community that have been interrupted several times. Iranian intransigence finally brought about the passage of a first Security Council resolution on July 31, 2006, in the form of an ultimatum opening the way to economic sanctions over which the great powers took several months to agree.

The Islamic Republic that came out of the 1979 revolution, a precursor of the international Islamist movement, now represents the only state-based threat to the West emanating from the Muslim world, since the Islamist danger generally assumes nonstate forms such as terror-

ism, armed militias, or political and religious militancy. Iran is, to be
sure, only a regional power, but the range of its activity, influence, and
capacity to harm—the Middle East and Central Asia—covers a region
that has been sensitive and vital enough to Western interests for decades
to elevate this regional status to the rank of a global strategic challenge.
The repercussions stemming from the 1979 Islamic revolution reaching
into the heart of the Western world for nearly thirty years are enough,
in themselves, to point to its geopolitical importance.[3]

The Iranian question encompasses at least four issues that are critical to global security, which Teheran's acquisition of nuclear capacity
would place in serious danger. The first is a natural consequence of the
concentration of the greater part of world energy reserves in the Middle East and Central Asia (Iran itself holds between 10 and 15 percent of
the world's oil and gas reserves), which has made this region the hunt-
ing ground of the great powers since the colonial era and today one of
the most nuclearized regions in the world (with India, Pakistan, Israel,
not to mention Russia, China, and the United States). Allowing Teheran to exercise nuclear blackmail on energy and thereby compromise
the stability of supplies represents an unacceptable risk for the West,
Russia, and now China. This risk is all the more serious because—and
this is the second aspect of the question—Iran has for decades aspired
to a role as a regional power, specifically as the dominant power in the
Persian Gulf and the Middle East. This was already true at the time
of the shah, who initiated the Iranian nuclear program with the help
of the Europeans, and was even more the case after the 1979 Islamic
revolution and the war with Iraq. Since the United States' elimination
of Sunni domination in Iraq and the weakening of moderate Arab regimes by Islamist movements, Iran no longer has any real rivals in the
Arab-Muslim world. Its regional hegemony would signify Persian and
Shiite Islam's stranglehold on the Middle East, that is, both radicalization of the region as a whole and perpetuation of Islam's internal
conflicts that foster the chronic instability of the Arab-Muslim world,
which is increasingly played out directly at the expense of the West.
This is why most Sunni Arab-Muslim countries—Saudi Arabia first in

line—are just as fearful as the United States and Europe of the establishment of a "Shiite arc" and the accession of the Islamic Republic to the ranks of the nuclear powers. Third, Iran's acquisition of a nuclear weapon would toll the death knell for the NPT, a pillar of the postwar international order already damaged by the North Korean nuclear test in the fall of 2006. Just as the North Korean crisis and China's much more significant rise to power risk leading to Japanese rearmament, including nuclear weapons, so Teheran's acquisition of the bomb would incite Saudi Arabia, Egypt, the Gulf states, and even Turkey to also acquire nuclear capability. The NPT and the International Atomic Energy Agency (IAEA) would not survive these developments. Finally, a nuclearized Iran would, even more than Saddam's Iraq, constitute a threat to the very existence of Israel, whose destruction is one of the objectives constantly proclaimed by the current Teheran government. This threat is no more acceptable to the West than it is to the Israelis.

The Iranian government has adroitly manipulated these various issues, using hostility to Israel both as a unifying element of the international Islamist movement and the "Arab street" for its benefit, beyond religious and ethnic differences, and as a test of Western determination to block its nuclear ambitions. The July 2006 war in Lebanon, provoked by Shiite Hezbollah with the active support of Iran and Syria, fit perfectly with this strategy, and neither Israel nor the international community missed the point. The resistance by the Party of God to the Israeli offensive nonetheless broadly served Teheran's aims: to make the Lebanese Shiite militia and its leader new heroes of radical Islam, to weaken the political structures of Lebanon, and to strengthen the Iranian position in its nuclear negotiations with the international community.

But, as is often the case, this tactical success might turn into a strategic defeat. The demonstration of Teheran's ability, through Hezbollah, to intervene in the Middle East conflict, to influence Lebanon's fate, and to secure the support of even its al Qaeda competitors ended up seriously troubling not only other Arab countries but also Russia and China, its traditional supporters in the Security Council. The international community's determination to stand up to the Iranian nuclear program and to the repeated provocations of President Ahmadinejad was only strengthened by the event. One year later, the lack of any progress in the negotiations and the new French government's increased determination to counter Teheran's nuclear ambitions escalated the tension. Yet, there is no easy resolution to this crisis, which is a test of the international community's ability to manage the challenges of proliferation in the new geopolitical landscape. In the face of the Iranian government's determination to acquire nuclear weapons—supported to some extent by Iranian public opinion for reasons of national pride but also for national security reasons—the only effective stance is an equal determination on the part of the international community to impose economic sanctions likely to hamper Iran's historical ambitions for power and thereby weaken the current government. In this optimistic scenario, when the time comes, Teheran would choose economic growth, political moderation, and cooperation with the West in exchange for recognition of its natural status as a regional power. On the other extreme, the pessimistic scenario would require the international community or, more likely, a coalition made up of the United States, Israel, and perhaps some European countries and a few Arab nations threatened by Teheran to intervene militarily to prevent an even more dangerous event: possession of a nuclear weapon by an extremist regime in the heart of the Middle East.

Iran will, in any event, be an influential regional power, and the positive or negative use it makes of that power will depend, in the short term, on the outcome of its confrontation with the international community on nuclear weapons, and in the longer term, on the evolution of its civil society, which is modern and Westernized, and of its domestic politics and diplomacy as well as the evolution of the region as a whole. Teheran can choose the path of economic catching up adopted by the major emerging countries and of cooperation with the West, even in the end of strategic reconciliation with Washington or, on the contrary, attempt to unify the Muslim world against America, Israel, and Europe. From this choice and its consequences will flow the future of a Middle East that has long been described as the world's powder keg.

THE RUSSIAN RECONQUISTA

Russia's return to the international stage presents very different challenges. After the collapse of the Soviet empire, the 1990s were first marked by a promising phase of political liberalization and economic reform, soon followed by the spread of corruption, domestic financial crisis, and political disorder, accompanied by withdrawal from the world diplomatic stage. Vladimir Putin's assumption of power in 2000 inaugurated a restoration of the Kremlin's authoritarian control over politics, the economy, and society, coupled with a sometimes aggressive reaffirmation of Russian claims to power over its periphery and on the international scene in response to a perceived Western tendency to encroach on its domestic affairs and area of influence. In both domestic and foreign spheres, Vladimir Putin's Russia seems on a backward track toward the old Russian/Soviet authoritarianism rather than going down the path to democratization and the market economy. This shift has created growing tension with the United States and Europe, once again reminiscent of the cold war, both with respect to the evolution of the regime itself and over energy matters, the Kremlin's policy toward countries on its western border, and U.S. antimissile defense plans.

The Russia of the first decade of this century has nonetheless not much in common with the world's former second superpower. Deprived of a large part of its geopolitical space and of the ideology that served as a pretext for its will to power, Russia is now an "emerging economy," with a weight comparable to that of Brazil, and is encountering more difficulty than others in integrating itself into the global economy. It will remain far behind the United States, the European Union, China, and India over the long term. It is suffering from a severe demographic decline—700,000 fewer people every year—and a drop in life expectancy that should reduce its population to about 100 million in

2050 (compared to 146 million in 2005), very far behind the other great powers. As for its military capabilities, despite recent shows of force, they are no longer comparable to those of the United States.

It is precisely in light of this loss of status and the humiliation it represents that the desire for reconquest that inspires the Kremlin and is the source of Vladimir Putin's wide domestic popularity should be understood. The general aim is again to draw even with the West, particularly with the great American rival, in international matters and to recapture some of the influence lost in its near abroad (Belarus, Ukraine, Moldova, and Georgia) and even in the Baltic states that are now members of the European Union. Beyond the Soviet era, with its mixed legacy, it is in fact the old Russian *grandeur*, glory, and power that Putin has pledged to restore. The means used for this restoration are an indissoluble mix of economic and political elements: the establishment of national energy and industrial powerhouses controlled by the Kremlin, the fight against demographic decline, rearmament, political manipulation of the energy weapon over countries dependent on Russian gas and oil supplies (former Soviet republics and the European Union in particular), support of client states or those providing raw materials for the national economy, often the unsavory former economic partners and political allies of the old USSR (Iran, Syria, Venezuela . . .), use of the veto power in the Security Council to influence the resolution of international crises (Iran, North Korea, Kosovo . . .), and anti-American rhetoric and alliances, particularly in the Middle East and Asia. With regard to the European Union, Moscow is conducting an ambivalent and opportunistic policy, relying on Europe, its principal trading partner, as a counterweight to Washington, while manipulating the EU's divisions on energy matters and taking satisfaction in the setbacks of European unification, as Europe's attractiveness on Ukraine and Georgia helps to undermine the Kremlin's influence. The EU's increasing dependency on Russian gas—30 percent of consumption by 2015—has provided Moscow with a powerful lever in this area.

Its geographical situation, its energy reserves, its seat as a permanent member of the Security Council, and its great past power all guarantee

Russia a key role at the heart of Eurasia, an unquestionably strategic area. Moscow will thus preserve a capacity for political influence and harm that is much greater than its present and future economic and military standing on the international stage. Its growing economic and political interdependence with the European Union, its demographic decline, and the pressure of China to its east and Islam to its south might in time bring Russia to establish closer ties with Europe in the form of an ambitious strategic partnership, which would be beneficial for international stability. This presupposes, however, coming to terms with the mutual distrust inherited from long before the four decades of the cold war, particularly for the new members of the European Union. Vladimir Putin's recent domestic and foreign policies have not followed this path. A more pessimistic scenario would, on the contrary, see Moscow affirm its "Eurasian calling" by establishing closer relations with Beijing, Teheran, and the dictatorships of Central Asia rather than with the democratic West. In any event, Russia no longer seems likely on its own to threaten the world geopolitical balance for the foreseeable future.

THE CHINESE UNKNOWN

China presents the most complex and paradoxical situation as regards its prospective geopolitical impact.[4] Unlike Iran, and even less than Russia, it is not engaged in any overt confrontation with any Western country, not even the United States since the improvement of relations in the aftermath of Richard Nixon's historic 1972 visit to Beijing. China has, quite the contrary, joined its rise to economic power with a policy of integration into the international system and an effort to settle its historic differences with neighboring countries, especially India. But, at the same time, because of the size of its population, its economic potential, and the military implications of both, the Middle Kingdom is the only state in the world likely to challenge the global strategic superiority of the United States in this century, that is, to upset the world strategic balance that has prevailed since 1945. Like Iran and Russia, China legitimately aspires to recover the grandeur and power that marked its thousand-year history until the humiliations inflicted by the West through the Opium Wars and the "unequal treaties" in the nineteenth century, by victorious Japan after the Sino-Japanese War, and the ensuing decline that lasted until the late 1970s. Thanks to its gigantic size and to the power of its economic takeoff, this ambition now seems within reach in the next few decades. This prospect provokes anxiety in Washington and Tokyo, the echo of an ancient fear of China in the West.

In response to this revived fear of future Chinese hegemony, Beijing has taken pains to present a doctrine of "peaceful rise" and "harmonious world," that is, a rise to power based on integration into the world economy and international institutions, with, as its principal goal, the well-being of a population soon to be 1.5 billion people to be achieved in a manner that is respectful of the common interest of mankind. At the opposite pole from the aggressive, predatory, and hegemonic attitude that accompanied the rise to power of Germany and Japan during the early decades of the twentieth century, followed by their downfall at the cost of two world wars, even unlike the worldwide ideological confrontation of the cold war, emerging China claims to be transcending ideological divisions—it is expert in the field—and to be working in favor of peace, development, and international cooperation.[5] Its model is supposed to be the peaceful rebirth of democratic Germany and Japan after the Second World War, even though democracy is not really on the agenda.

This language is unquestionably based on solid facts. It is clear first of all that Beijing's current aim is exclusively the country's economic and social development, and Chinese leaders never fail to point out, correctly, that this represents a formidable challenge, considering its size, its population, and its lack of natural resources. China is still today a developing country with low per capita income whose economy is only one-seventh the size of that of the United States and one-third that of Japan. This aim has, to be sure, led to a global, opportunistic, and unscrupulous pursuit of raw materials, which has given rise to tensions and other perverse geopolitical effects, but the economic development of the country is still the guiding principle of Chinese diplomacy.

This economic rise has also been accompanied since the late 1970s by China's gradual integration into international political and economic institutions (the UN, the Bretton Woods institutions, Asian regional organizations, full membership of the WTO in 2001), its signing of some international disarmament treaties, and the settlement of border disputes with its Indian and Vietnamese neighbors, with the notable exception of the dispute with Japan over gas and oil reserves in the China Sea and other maritime disputes. Except in the area of human rights, Tibet, and in respect of the nature of its political regime, China has relaxed traditional sensitivities about its sovereignty.

Nonetheless, questions about the possible implications of the Chinese rise to power are not only legitimate but clearly indispensable for the West, and they are of as much concern to Europe as to the United States. The first reason to be concerned is that any political and military domination is based on economic power, and that history offers conversely few examples of nations—much less empires—whose economic power did not have strategic and military consequences. Beijing's current concentration on economic development is, therefore, in no way incompatible with more long-term strategic aims, which will in any event naturally arise from its foreseeable status as a world economic superpower, as was the case for the United States in the twentieth century. The all-out search for the mineral and energy resources necessary for economic development has already led to competition on a global scale and to opportunistic diplomacy, often opposed to Western policies, values, and interests, with regard to Iran, Sudan, and Venezuela in particular. In the course of 2006, for example, Beijing engaged in worldwide diplomatic activity of an intensity unprecedented in the history of modern China and with no equivalent on the part of other powers, including the United States. Official visits to Washington, New Delhi, Islamabad, and many countries of Africa, Central Asia, Latin America, and the Middle East, Asian regional summits, and anti-American forums allowed China to display its new status as a world superpower. The purpose of this international activism was primarily to make certain of supplies of hydrocarbons and raw materials, but it also involved the extension of the Chinese sphere of influence and its economic presence well beyond the Far East, through diverse forms of cooperation, without any conditionality and interference of any kind in the practices or policies of the beneficiary governments. When a historic summit assembling the leaders of forty-eight African nations was held in Beijing in November 2006, the West woke up to the geopolitical stakes of Chinese presence on the continent, involving much more than competition for oil and raw materials. The intensity of trade relations between China and corrupt, if not criminal, states has undermined the efforts of the international community to reform African "governance," a condition for the continent's economic takeoff, as well as its efforts to enforce respect for human rights. The support of many African votes in international organizations will also help Beijing place its representatives in key positions. In addition to the exchange of raw materials for inexpensive products, the development of infrastructures, financing of projects, and technical assistance will soon make China the new colonial power in Africa, at the expense of the Western powers and without the occasional virtues sometimes seen in colonialism. There is perfect harmony between the necessities of economic development and diplomatic rivalry with the other great powers.

Beijing has in fact not hidden its legitimate ambition to play a major role on the international stage, already demonstrated in its involvement in the North Korean and Iranian nuclear crises, in which it has been an essential participant. In both cases, moreover, Chinese concern to maintain the status quo to ensure the safety of its Middle Eastern oil supplies and avoid a direct confrontation with the United States in East Asia finally led Beijing to adopt Western positions, having made sure to defend its economic and political interests beforehand. In the eyes of its Asian neighbors, the growth of China signals a major strategic shift, a source of anxiety for Japan and, in other Asian countries, of a diplomatic balancing act among the rival powers of the region: the United States, Japan, China, India, and Russia.

These concerns are further justified by the fact that this rise to power has extended to the military sphere. The Chinese defense budget has been constantly growing since the beginnings of the policy of modernization and has had a double digit annual growth rate since 1990. Estimated to be about 140 billion dollars by American military experts (much higher than the official figure of 45 billion for 2007), it is now thought to be the third largest in the world, after those of the United States and Russia, and 3.5 times larger than that of Japan. The Pentagon's 2005 annual report on the state of Chinese forces thus warned against the strengthening of Beijing's military capabilities, a threat for Taiwan, Japan, India, and even the United States itself, still the principal military power in the region. The modernization of Chinese forces is aimed, in the first place, at maintaining pressure on Taiwan, whose independence Beijing intends to prevent, and at securing energy supply lines, which are vital for China's development. Seven hundred missiles are thus permanently targeted on Taiwan, and the reinforcement of Chinese naval war capabilities in the Indian Ocean to secure energy supply lines is on the agenda. But the modernization of Chinese military capabilities has also extended to the development of strategic missiles able to reach targets across the Pacific, to antimissile defense, experimented successfully in early 2007 against a used satellite, and to an ambitious space and satellite program with undoubted military spinoffs. While Pentagon hawks invoking the "Chinese threat" remain in the minority, China's military revival has now awakened the attention of most Western experts.

Several considerations, however, make it advisable to place the rise of Chinese military power and the hypothesis of an evolution of Beijing toward hegemony in perspective. Historically, even under the messianic reign of Mao Zedong and during the worst hours of the cold war, China was involved only in very limited border conflicts and adopted a pragmatic attitude in its confrontation with Taiwan. The burden of the past, particularly the memory of humiliations inflicted by the West in the nineteenth century and of Japanese aggression, and a powerful feeling of vulnerability to the United States—with its military budget ten times the size of that of China—on the contrary foster a certain paranoia that has given Chinese rearmament an at least partially defensive character toward other regional powers, notably Washington. Even powerful militarily, China would thus not necessarily have hegemonic or aggressive inclinations and would not have the means to catch up with the United States.

A second consideration has to do with the fragility of Chinese economic development, on which the country's military power ultimately depends. This fragility results from the demographic factor and the social problems it engenders, from the divide between urban and industrial China and rural China, from environmental risks, and from many other uncertainties relating to the current pace and model for growth of the Chinese economy. China might very well, if not implode, not become, in the next few decades at least, the economic superpower most analysts anticipate, and economic disappointments of this kind would necessarily have a moderating influence on the country's military capabilities and Beijing's willingness to use them.

The most persuasive consideration in the end, even if China had become an economic power comparable to the United States, brings to the fore the pacifying virtues of integration into the world economy, more specifically the interdependence of the two future giants of global geopolitics. The priority given to economic development has led Beijing to favor international stability and to avoid any serious confrontation with the United States, Japan, and Taiwan. On the economic plane, China's rise, the international opening on which it is based, and its energy supplies have created very heavy dependence on the outside world and owe a good deal to American goodwill. Conversely, the American economy is increasingly dependent, for its imports, the profitability of its investments, and the financing of its massive deficits, on the strength of Chinese economic growth. As a consequence, Washington has no real interest in hampering the economic takeoff of China and, conversely, China would suffer from a real confrontation with the United States. Strategically, whereas Washington is rightly or wrongly worried by China's rise, Beijing fears that the United States, which has the means to do so, will seek to thwart its economic development. China's enlightened self-interest is, therefore, to cooperate with America. Reciprocally, Washington more and more needs Beijing's support in the fight against terrorism and nuclear proliferation, the resolution of the North Korean and Iranian crises, and the stabilization of Iraq and the Middle East.

It is thus entirely conceivable that relations between China and the United States, which will shape the twenty-first century, will turn toward a global partnership based on shared enlightened self-interest and Beijing's growing assumption of responsibility, a solid guarantee for the stability of the international system. But it cannot be ruled out that this objective alliance will last only through the long transition at the end of which America will have to share its status as global superpower with China: after all, isn't it easier today to anticipate a future confrontation between the United States and China than it must have been in the early years of the twentieth century to imagine the devastation produced by Nazism and Soviet hegemony? China's rise to power might also trigger autonomous defensive reactions from other powers, such as Japan, Russia, or India, as well as from America itself, with repercussions that would be hard to control. Like Chinese ambivalence between strength and weakness, Western policy toward China's spectacular awakening will, therefore, have to continue to combine active support for its integration into the world economy and the international system, on the one hand, and vigilance and preservation of ultimate strategic superiority, on the other. This kind of dualism is all the more called for because, while no power in the world is likely to be in a position to challenge American strategic leadership in the coming decades, the alliance of Moscow, Beijing, Teheran, and a few other dictatorships in challenging American domination and the Atlantic Alliance is already a rhetorical and political reality.

The ambition of "countering American hegemony" is expressed with varying degrees of virulence from Moscow through Teheran to Beijing, but it is a constant refrain in the diplomacy of the three countries. The Shanghai Cooperation Organization (SCO), a regional forum established in 1996 on Beijing's initiative, bringing together China, Russia, and several totalitarian republics of Central Asia rich in energy resources, such as Uzbekistan and Tajikistan, gave some substance to this alliance by inviting Iranian President Ahmadinejad in June 2006 and admitting Teheran as an observer, in the midst of the international confrontation over Iranian nuclear power and on the eve of Hezbollah's attacks on Israel. Initially dedicated to the fight against Islamist terror, the SCO is in the process of turning itself into an anti-American and anti-Atlanticist political and military alliance among its member states, particularly the two former centers of the Communist bloc, as confirmed by the August 2007 meeting of the organization. Already active in the areas of energy and diplomacy, cooperation between Moscow and Beijing would then take a strategic turn, which would not fail to increase tensions and crystallize the reawakened antagonism between the democratic West and nationalistic or religious authoritarian regimes united against it under the banner of the new Russian-Chinese partnership. Similarly, closer relations between China and a fundamentalist Iran dominating the Middle East—its principal oil supplier in 2006—or with Pakistan—which it secretly helped to become a nuclear power—against India would be very troublesome for peace and security.

Even in a less extreme scenario, Moscow and Beijing clearly share the ambition to establish around themselves, with the help of traditional or occasional allies of the United States such as India, South Korea, and Pakistan, a pole of power competing with the Atlantic community on the world diplomatic stage, and it is also clear that this aim is already within their grasp.

Hence the geopolitics of globalization has placed the United States, Europe, and the Western democracies face to face with three questions in the form of challenges. How should the United States best deal with China's rise to power? How can the democratic West maintain its ultimate strategic superiority in the face of the possibility of a totalitarian hegemony of whatever stripe, but also, and more important, preserve its political leadership for the purpose of preventing such an eventuality? How can Europe avoid being marginalized in a world that is likely to be organized around an American-Asian duopoly?

4

THE WEST ON TRIAL

The difficulties of the West, as we have seen, represent one of the paradoxical sequels of the end of the bipolar world in the threefold form of the erosion of Atlantic solidarity, a relative decline in American global influence, and the stalling of European integration. We thus need to determine whether these difficulties are temporary or lasting and, more fundamentally, whether the transatlantic partnership is still the best, if not the only, option for the United States and Europe in the world of the twenty-first century.

In 2002–2003, at the height of the transatlantic crisis over Iraq, questions raised about the future of Western solidarity produced three kinds of answers. In the view of the optimists and the diplomats, the strength of the values and interests shared by the New World and the Old would, as in the past, overcome the turbulence caused by the Iraqi crisis. Conversely, the "separatist" argument emphasized the growing divergence between Europe and the United States, including political and cultural matters, and predicted, often with some satisfaction, the deepening of the Atlantic rift as a true divorce. The future of the Atlantic partnership, however, may well lie between these two positions: in a middle way that recognizes the structural challenges that the post–cold war, post-September 11 world poses to Atlantic solidarity but also

takes into account the renewed necessity of the Euro-American partnership and of an active commitment on its behalf in the new geopolitical context. Since the second Bush administration, even though the
"divorce" advocates have not disarmed, realism has prevailed in both
governments and public opinion, fostered by the twin failures of the
American intervention in Iraq and the European constitutional project
as well as by the recognition of new forms of solidarity between the
two sides of the Atlantic in the world to come. The state of transatlantic relations has thus substantially improved since the dramatic
confrontation of 2002 and 2003. Nevertheless, that crisis was severe
enough, and the misunderstandings behind it lasting enough, to war-
rant further analysis.

TWOFOLD BLINDNESS

America and Europe entered the twenty-first century singing different
and indeed discordant melodies. The disappearance of the Communist
threat at the beginning of the 1990s opened a period of questioning
about the future of the Atlantic Alliance and begun the process of dis-
tancing its two centers from one another, encouraging self-satisfaction
and arrogance on the part of the American superpower and driving
the European Union toward pacifism and an anti-Americanism closely linked to its own identity crisis. When the Iraqi conflict arose, the
trauma inflicted on the American people by the September 11 attacks
and the long period during which European politicians and public opinion underestimated the impact of that event transformed what could
have remained a mere difference of opinion into a deep and devastating
breakdown of mutual trust.

The gap between collective perceptions on both sides of the Atlantic
became, in 2003, the source of the most serious challenge experienced
by Western solidarity since the Second World War. Had it not been
for the shock of September 11, the first George W. Bush administration
would never have been able to secure near unanimous American public

support for its unilaterally decided preventive military action against the regime of Saddam Hussein under the banner of the "global war on terror." Had European public opinion not misunderstood the impact of September 11 on the American psyche and the international system, France and Germany under Jacques Chirac and Gerhard Schröder would probably not have found it politically opportune to divide Europe and the West by transforming principled opposition to intervention in Iraq, however legitimate and sensible it might have been, into a French-German-Russian campaign against the foreign policy of Europe's indispensable ally. Had it not been for shared blindness about the new fragility of the Atlantic partnership in the post–cold war era, the first Bush administration and its French and German partners of the time would not have taken the risk of treating it so recklessly.

However mistaken public opinion views may have been, it is the political leaders who exploited and manipulated them on both sides of the Atlantic who bear responsibility for this joint diplomatic disaster. The Bush administration made a series of mistakes of serious consequences. The first was to make the "global war on terror" the keystone of American foreign policy after September 11, as this concept is too narrow in view of the United States' many interests in the world, too abstract to be operational, but also because it disregards the causes and political motives of terrorism in favor of a Manichaean and simplistic military approach that has no chance of eliminating the roots of the problem. By focusing the greater part of its military response to the September 11 attacks on Iraq, Washington then went after the wrong enemy, diverted precious resources from the fight against terrorism in Afghanistan and elsewhere, and, even more seriously, increased the terrorist threat by providing al Qaeda with a new "failed state" in the heart of the Middle East where it could reconstitute its operational bases. Moreover, by launching the Iraq operation unilaterally and with no real evidence for the existence of weapons of mass destruction, the United States alienated the international community, strengthening the resentment against it already prevalent in the Arab-Muslim world and elsewhere. This hostility was deepened, and American moral prestige tarnished, by American military abuses in Iraq and other violations of human rights in the name of the war on terrorism, in Guantanamo and in the CIA's secret prisons. Finally, Washington committed the sin of incompetence in its conduct of the war and the stabilization process in Iraq. By not deploying the resources necessary to control the chaos arising from its controversial intervention, America further clouded its aura as a global superpower, already grown dim in the eyes of its many adversaries, as well as in those of its allies by its inability to prevent the September 11 attacks.

With its ever increasing tribute in human lives (over four thousand American soldiers as at the beginning of 2008 and tens of thousands of Iraqi victims of the civil war), its staggering financial cost (over $400 billion by April 2007), its no less immense diplomatic damage, and its at best mixed results aside from the removal of Saddam Hussein, the Iraq adventure has had a devastating impact on the United States' prestige and leadership in the world. Even if it is too soon to make a serious assessment of the results of the war against al Qaeda and its followers, American involvement in Iraq nonetheless diverted Washington from the stabilization of Afghanistan and Pakistan, dealing with the North Korean and Iranian nuclear threats, the resolution of the Israeli-Palestinian conflict, and the rise to power of China and Russia, that is, the principal strategic challenges facing the international community.

This sorry balance sheet only partially—and only retrospectively—redeems the mistakes committed on the European side. We have already underlined how long it took for governments and public opinion to realize the actual significance of the September 11 attacks and all the developments that had made them possible. On a continent traditionally inclined to the status quo and naive optimism, the European experience of terrorism paradoxically contributed to a misunderstanding that had weighty consequences, allowing Europeans to believe that the destruction of the Twin Towers and the attack on the Pentagon were of the same nature, if not the same magnitude, as terrorist actions committed earlier in Europe. This analogy ignored that the operation launched by al Qaeda constituted the first act of asymmetrical warfare, of the weak against the strong, and inaugurated an era in which the worst has indeed become possible, as a result of a global political strategy based on hyperterrorism and the increasing dissemination of weapons of mass destruction.

This initial blindness as to the way the world had changed on September 11, 2001, opened the way to a second European mistake, this one political: the international campaign against Washington led by the Paris-Berlin-Moscow axis in the months preceding the invasion of Iraq, against a background of a European public opinion under the influence of a mix of pacifism and anti-Americanism. To be sure, "the French were right," as the American liberal media eventually recognized, in their warnings against the risks of civil war and chaos that would result from the end of Saddam's dictatorship. The most costly mistake made by some European governments thus did not have to do with the substance but with the form and intensity of the opposition of the Chirac-Schröder-Putin trio to the invasion of Iraq. A pure and simple refusal to participate in the Iraq adventure, after vainly attempting to dissuade an ally from undertaking it, would have been perfectly legitimate and acceptable to the United States government and American public opinion. But the lobbying campaign conducted among African members of the Security Council to block the proposed Anglo-American resolution, the threat of a French veto, and other steps aimed at thwarting the American plan went well beyond simple abstention. It was this excess in opposition on the part of historic allies, on a subject rightly or wrongly viewed as involving the vital interests of the United States—and not the mere refusal to participate in the war—that cost France, and Germany to a lesser extent, a huge loss of esteem in the hearts of Americans. Several years later, many Europeans are still unaware of this important nuance and invoke the legitimacy of disagreements among allies, while failing to see that an alliance also imposes a certain moderation in the expression of such disagreements.

Not satisfied with making the American people feel betrayed, the Paris-Berlin-Moscow axis of 2003 also divided the governments of the European Union and alienated the future members from Central Eastern and Europe—historically weary about Russia and a pro-Russian German leadership—precisely on this question of principle regarding the duty of solidarity inherent in any alliance, rather than on the appropriateness of the war itself. The first Bush administration, of course, poured oil on the fire by contrasting "old Europe"—protectionist and anti-American—to "new Europe"—market-oriented and Atlanticist. These internal divisions ensured the absence of the European Union from a debate with major consequences for the evolution of the international system, confirming in passing Europe's inability to construct itself in schizophrenic opposition to its American ally.

While the opposition to the war of an overwhelming majority of European public opinion had its primary root in a pacifist and conservative view of the international order, the French and German opposition to Washington was based on the openly declared promotion of a "multipolar world" in which new power centers—with Europe in the lead—would form a counterweight to the American superpower. An objective of this kind had the twofold advantage of easily establishing a consensus in the international community—thereby guaranteeing its advocates worldwide popularity—and at the same time satisfying the French and European inclination to make opposition to the United States an element of their identity, if not an existential necessity. Ill advised with respect to both international legitimacy and strategic cogency, the Iraqi invasion no doubt appeared to Paris and Berlin as a historic opportunity to assert, with the Kremlin's cooperation, a European center of power as a counterweight to Washington's hazardous unilateralism at a crucial moment in the redefinition of the post–cold war international order.

But, again, this was to pay the high price of a strategic illusion and a diplomatic fault for a mere tactical success. The multipolar state of today's world is an objective reality that can only become more pronounced, for better or worse, as we head into the twenty-first century. As such, it needs no encouragement. The desire of some for a multipolar world reflects in reality a nostalgia for power in the face of postwar American hegemony and, beyond that, a traditional vision of international relations focused, on the one hand, on nation-states (with no regard for their democratic or authoritarian character) and based, on the other, on the old theories of balance of power and the "concert of nations" that governed Europe in the nineteenth century with all too obvious consequences. Faithful in this respect to the Gaullist tradition, the vision of a multipolar world advocated by Jacques Chirac was perfectly consistent with a certain fascination for great nations burdened with history, such as Russia or China, however undemocratic they may be, and with the aspiration to establish privileged ties between them and that other great nation, France, with the common purpose of building a counterweight to American power. It is easy to understand, therefore, that the promotion of a multipolar world is displeasing to Washington, especially when used as a doctrine to support a foreign policy in open conflict with Washington.

Finally, and most important, Europeans have less interest than anyone else in the advent of a multipolar world in which the most powerful democracy in the world—the guarantor of the stability of the planet—would be contained and held in check by new powers that are undemocratic and potentially hegemonic. Because of its economic, demographic, and military weakness, the "European pole" is the one that is likely to suffer most from the worldwide redistribution of economic and strategic power arising from globalization. And if the history of the twentieth century bears a single lesson, it is that of the indispensability of the ultimate strategic supremacy of democratic nations in a world in which power will be disseminated around the globe as never before, with unprecedented means of mass destruction. Beyond symbolic satisfaction, head-on opposition to the American ally in the name of a multipolar world thus did not make much sense from the very standpoint of enlightened European self-interest. This is all the more true since, after reveling in challenging Washington on the international stage, the Europeans—with France in the lead—found nothing better to do than to undermine the project of a political Europe by rejecting a constitutional treaty that was intended to form its minimalist foundation. This rejection derived from the same blindness: while the world is being reshaped at lightning speed, often to the detriment of the Old Continent, Europeans got lost in untimely and largely irrelevant debates, only to prohibit themselves in the end from taking the small step forward that a European Constitution would have represented.

TACTICAL RECONCILIATION OR STRATEGIC TURNING POINT?

The crisis in transatlantic relations triggered by the invasion of Iraq has had at least the virtue of bringing underlying tensions to the surface and demonstrating to its protagonists the appropriate degree of restraint. Since 2004 and the reelection of George W. Bush, and even more so since the subsequent change of leadership in Germany and France, the time has come for reconciliation between the United States and Europe and for Washington's return to multilateralism. This development is primarily the result of the lessons drawn on both sides from the destructive confrontation of 2002 and 2003. Washington has had the increasingly bitter experience, as its setbacks in Iraq have continued, of the price of arrogance and the political and military limitations of unilateralism and coalitions of the willing in the uncertain geopolitical context of the early twenty-first century. On all the major international issues—from North Korea to Iran, the Middle East, and Darfur—the UN Security Council has resumed its role as the natural theater for diplomacy and the handling of international crises. The Europeans, for their part, have assessed the political cost of head-on opposition to Washington, both with regard to European cohesion as well as Atlantic solidarity. They have filled in the initial gap between them and the United States in terms of awareness of the world-changing effects of the September 11 attacks and buried, in Madrid, London, and Copenhagen, any illusion of European immunity in the face of terrorism and fundamentalism. Disregard of offenses on both sides and transatlantic reconciliation thus became a shared priority not only for the reelected American president and the new German chancellor Angela Merkel but also for French diplomacy long before the election of Nicolas Sarkozy.

Shortly after taking the oath of office for the second time, George W. Bush came to Brussels in February 2005 to meet with representatives of the European institutions, unprecedented evidence of Washington's new awareness of the EU's existence and political usefulness. Europeans and Americans, Washington and Paris in particular, have since then acted in concert on most major international issues, notably those having to do with the Middle East: Lebanon's emancipation from Syria, the Iranian nuclear negotiations, the attitude vis-à-vis Hamas coming to power in the Palestinian territories, and efforts toward a cease-fire between Israel and Hezbollah in the summer of 2006. Even on sensitive subjects such as the process of political restoration and economic reconstruction in Iraq, moderation and cooperation have been prevalent on both sides. In response to American and Japanese concerns about the security of Taiwan, the European Union also decided not to lift its embargo on arms sales to China for the sake of improving trade relations with Beijing.

It is, however, legitimate to question the real depth and durability of this reconciliation, particularly in light of the recent debates about the growing transatlantic rift between Europe and the United States, the structural challenges objectively facing the Atlantic partnership, and the temptation to follow alternative paths that has occasionally surfaced on both sides of the Atlantic.[1] The driving force underlying the crisis of 2002 and 2003 was indeed the temptation, in Washington as well as Paris and Berlin, to turn one's back on the Atlantic Alliance in favor of other strategic partnerships perhaps considered better suited to the future international balance of power. American neoconserva-

tives made no mystery of their contempt for Europe and their convic-
tion that the Atlantic Alliance was obsolete. They intended to replace
NATO with ad hoc coalitions of the willing put together according to
the mission at hand, sometimes with allies of convenience, whether or
not they were democratic and even though their reliability might be
questionable. The fundamental concept of the centrality of the Euro-
American relationship and of the necessary unity of the West for the
stability of the world and the security of the United States was thus
called into question at the highest level. Similarly, in Europe, traditional
French rivalry with America and the more recent fear felt by German
pacifists toward a superpower that had become difficult to restrain
brought about the renewal of old temptations to seek alternative alliances: in the direction of the European Union itself, a potential counterweight to American power, as well as Russia and other emerging
powers with which Europe might have an interest in establishing strategic partnerships without, if not against, the United States. In the face
of the anticipated prospect of the "breakdown of the American order,"
was it not in Europe's interest to look toward Asia and the East where
the United States itself had such a strong presence?[2]

On both sides of the Atlantic, however, even more so in Washington than in Europe, these temptations were subjected to the salutary
test of reality, namely, the cardinal importance of solid and sustainable alliances, those based on a true community of political and moral
values and economic and strategic interests, something all the more
important in the uncertain multipolar world now taking shape. By
this standard, Europe has no real ally other than the United States and
vice versa. This temporarily ignored reality principle ensures that the
transatlantic reconciliation of recent years is strategic and long lasting.
This does not mean that the EU, following the example of the United
States and to the extent it can, should not establish closer relations with
other great powers, particularly China and India, where it has too little
influence, as well as with its unavoidable Russian neighbor. But these
relations between powers are different in nature than the fundamental solidarity that has united Western democracies for two centuries

in a common destiny. It is not without one another, much less against one another, that Europe and America will ensure the preservation of peace, democracy, and their own security in the world of the twenty-first century.

The growing anxiety of American public opinion about the country getting bogged down in Iraq, its vulnerability to terrorism, its international isolation, and the rise of anti-Americanism in the world, much as the weariness of Europeans about a confrontation with America in the context of a multifaceted deterioration of world affairs, expresses that common awareness and probably explains the parallel change in direction of diplomacy and public opinion. In this sense, the improvement in transatlantic relations that was initiated in 2004 unquestionably has a defensive tone to it. Terrorism, of course, is not the substitute for the Soviet threat that some would like to see as the new cement for the Atlantic bond. But the new geopolitical era marked by the emergence of new undemocratic powers and multiple risks, and the concomitant weakening of the Western bloc, is certainly capable of triggering a renewal of Atlantic solidarity. Far from a superficial and precarious reconciliation on the path to the predicted great divorce, the post-Iraq warming of transatlantic relations may well represent the initial step in a long-term trend that would see Europe and the United States converge in a much deeper way than in the past, including at the time of the cold war, in order to preserve their positions before attempting to recover their shared leadership in the world of the twenty-first century. The prospects for such a convergence have been significantly improved with the accession to power of Angela Merkel in Germany and Nicolas Sarkozy in France. Both do not view Europe's primary function as being a counterweight to American power, but rather as being a relevant, if demanding, partner and ally. Both share a strategic vision closer to that of Washington and place Atlantic solidarity on higher ground than occasional differences over specific issues.

Yet, the fact remains that this improvement is starting from a position of weakness—the twofold crisis of American leadership and European integration—which must be overcome. A renewed Atlantic partnership makes no sense unless it brings together an America that has restored its credibility and its capacity for international action and a Europe that has become a real player on the world stage. The issue then becomes whether these two threshold conditions can still be met.

THE NEW AMERICAN CHALLENGE

Most major analysts of American foreign policy, from Joseph Nye to Henry Kissinger, agree in concluding that the strategic superiority of the United States is not likely to be challenged by any competitor in the next few decades. Only China is seen as a possible long-term rival, alone or in partnership with other adversaries of Washington, such as Iran and Russia. It can, however, be taken for granted that America will do what is necessary to maintain its advance and its superiority, demonstrated by the staggering size of the Pentagon's budget and the development of antimissile defense systems. The same is true in the economic sphere, where the dynamism of its form of capitalism, its mastery of the technologies of the future, its position as the world's university, and the renewal of its population will enable America to keep itself in the first rank, whereas China and the other emerging countries will have to confront huge economic, social, political, and environmental challenges. The United States' principal problem today has to do with the decline of its leadership and the weakening of its soft power on the international stage, the reduction of its room for strategic and diplomatic maneuver as a result of getting bogged down in Iraq, and the rise of anti-Americanism throughout the world. More specifically, Washington has lost a good deal of its influence in the Middle East and of its aura in Europe and Latin America, is stuck in a conflictual relationship with the Arab-Muslim world, is losing ground to China in the Far East and Africa, and has had to let Europe and China take the lead in dealing with Iranian and North Korean nuclear proliferation. The two major axes of American foreign policy since September 11, 2001—the war against terrorism and the democratization of the Middle East—are controversial both conceptually and in their implementation and have produced mixed if not negative results, further discredited by the fiasco in Iraq. Majorities in most of the forty-seven nations surveyed by the Pew Research Center in 2007 expressed suspicion about both these pillars of recent United States foreign policy.

To recover its status as a respected superpower in a world that has become multipolar, unpredictable, and unquestionably more dangerous, America has to rethink its foreign policy and its global role, both shaken since the end of the confrontation between East and West. While the cold war made it the uncontested leader of the "free world" and the ultimate guarantor of peace and democracy in the face of the Communist threat, the elimination of that threat and its promotion to sole superpower status have been less beneficial to America. They have encouraged long-standing tendencies toward self-centeredness, arrogance, and unilateralism in foreign policy and other dealings with the rest of the planet precisely at a time when global attitudes vis-à-vis America's role in the world and the global balance of power were about to change. For a variety reasons analyzed in the preceding chapters, America's unipolar moment in the 1990s has produced widespread negative feelings, ranging from resentment and hatred in the Arab-Muslim world to a mere eagerness to compete and defend different values and collective preferences in Europe, Latin America, and parts of Asia. The paradoxical mix of unilateralism and failure of the George W. Bush era in foreign policy has dramatically strengthened these negative feelings and brought the "indispensable nation" down from its messianic pedestal, even among the most pro-American of Washington's allies. In addition to this emotional dimension, the balance of power is objectively shifting toward a multipolar world in which new emerging continentwide nations have become indispensable contributors to the solution of most global or regional issues, be it security crises, climate change, or economic imbalances.

Paradoxically, for all its aura as the champion of globalization and multiculturalism, adjusting to a globalized multipolar world in which civil societies and public opinion have an increasing influence on governments and world affairs represents a particularly difficult challenge for the United States after decades of uncontested global dominance. While the first Bush administration's unilateralism went radically the wrong way, recognizing that America will need to compose with other economic and strategic powers in the world to come, that its society, values, and political agenda cannot be permanently at odds with those of the rest of the world, that, as the strongest global power, it has to contribute to the resolution of global concerns is likely to require significant time and political wisdom.

As a return to the isolationism of the 1920s is no longer an option, incompatible as it is with the global spread of American power, the challenge this represents has been accurately analyzed by Zbigniew Brzezinski in terms of a choice between domination and leadership.[3] It is clear that American power will have more difficulty exercising either one in the future than it did during the bipolar period of the cold war or its unipolar aftermath. But it is easier to induce acceptance of leadership than of domination. The rest of the world has in fact always asked a good deal of America, both power and effectiveness, without which nothing would be possible, but also vision, generosity, justice, and ethics, necessary to shape consensus and resolve conflicts peacefully. This cocktail of virtues defines the leadership that made *pax americana* possible during much of the second half of the twentieth century and that Washington is now duty bound to restore.

The United States is thus confronted, in a specific form dictated by its present position as the only global superpower, with a choice comparable to that facing all the other principal actors on the international stage: on one side, domination, aimed primarily at guaranteeing its own security everywhere in the world, chiefly through military means, on the other, leadership, that integrates national security within a larger enterprise of reconstructing an international order based on a global community of interests bringing together all participants of goodwill.

The choice of leadership would presuppose no longer making the "war on terror"—controversial both conceptually and in respect of its doctrinal corollaries such as preventive war and coalitions of the willing—the alpha and omega of American foreign policy. To be consen-

sual and legitimate, external action by the world's greatest power must
not be limited to guaranteeing its own security and that of its allies, but
have the broader goal of taking on the principal challenges of the planet, including terrorism, but also global warming, poverty, ethnic conflicts, nuclear proliferation, chaos in the Middle East, and the decline
of multilateralism. America will recover its legitimacy when it adopts
the aim of rebuilding in a concerted way with the rest of the world
an international order for the twenty-first century. The time has come
for a realistic rethinking of American foreign policy along those lines,
which remains to be done. While the 2004 past presidential election
was won on national security grounds, that of November 2008 may
well partly focus instead on restoring American leadership and credit
in the world.

THE END OF EUROPE?

Europe faces an even more formidable challenge. In a sad paradox, at
the very moment when globalization is intensifying and continental
powers are emerging, making further European integration increasingly necessary for the Union's member states, the EU has stumbled, the
victim of public disenchantment. While governments and the media
have tended to focus their attention on the fate of the EU constitutional
treaty, its rejection in the spring of 2005 by two of the founding states of
the European Community was much more the result of a deep underlying crisis than the true cause of the current stagnation. It is therefore
important to focus on an analysis of that crisis and, beyond that, on the
historical situation of the European project. We have already emphasized the intrinsic causes: a doubling of the size of the Union without
reinforcement of its institutions, a loss of effectiveness and, more important, of purpose resulting from the growing heterogeneity in the
abilities and ambitions of ever more numerous member states, and the
gradual disappearance of the founding generation of political leaders.
But the crisis of the European project also has an external dimension
that has not been very thoroughly explored: the change in geopolitical

paradigm at the turn of the twenty-first century has imperceptibly set European unification even more out of step with its environment than it already was. The fall of the Berlin Wall had already shaken the foundations of the European Community by eliminating the confrontation between East and West that had been its breeding ground and by compelling the entry of the "other Europe" into the club. But the new era on which we have embarked since 2001 has challenged the very ideology of European unification and put into question its relevance for the continent in the world to come.

The European Community was built on two fundamental pillars: peace through the transcendence of nationalism and narrow views of sovereignty and integration through law and the market economy. It was also based on the assumed stability of the international environment, which fit with the cold war and American military protection, sparing European nations from any strategic concerns. In this sense the European project was indeed a child of the Atlantic era and the *pax americana* and even more of the astrategic world that reached its peak between the economic recovery of the mid 1980s and the end of the technological euphoria of the 1990s. To the extent that it paid attention to the rest of the world, Europe defended elsewhere its own values and the transposition of its own model, that is, multilateralism, the limitation of sovereign powers by international law, an unlimited faith in the virtues of dialogue and negotiation for the resolution of conflicts, and a parallel aversion for the use of force.

But the characteristics of the new international environment have considerably intensified the atypical nature of the European project, giving rise to an increasingly problematic gap between it and the rest of the world. The first change has, of course, been the return of history, that is, of strategic concerns and interests, of power relations, of war and mass terrorism as driving forces of the international system in a world in the process of being radically reshaped. Multilateralism, global governance through law, and pacifism—Europe's ideological baggage—have undergone a parallel retreat. A corollary to this transformation has been the renewed strength of the ideology of sovereignty and nationalism, including within the EU, precisely where the European credo had preached their disappearance.[4] Both old and new powers at the beginning of this century are nations with cultures decidedly attached to notions of sovereignty: the United States, of course, which offered the world multilateralism without ever abdicating its own sovereignty in the face of the constraints of that stance, as well as China, India, Russia, Japan, Iran, Israel, Venezuela—and in truth almost all the nations of the world in their quest for power or simply for identity. The reaffirmation of the ideology of sovereignty and nationalism has, of course, spread to the Old Continent itself—its birthplace—as European integration started to unravel. England and France had never really given them up, and the states of Eastern and Southern Europe—recently liberated from Soviet domination, dictatorship, or a federal straitjacket imposed from outside—have found in them their identity and freedom. Even within the traditionally most Euro-federalist states, such as the Netherlands and Belgium, fears of loss of identity and disturbances of the social fabric produced by globalization, immigration, and advances in European unification itself have fostered nationalist (or even regionalist in the case of Belgium) regression and a populist upsurge.

Finally, the European Union can no longer think of itself exclusively as a "single market" and a haven of peace and idealism in an open world governed by realpolitik and torn with conflict. Globalization makes it impossible to build any economic or strategic sanctuary: whether in matters of economic and cultural exchanges, energy supplies, migratory flows, terrorist risks, or the question of its own frontiers, Europe is fully immersed in the great global ocean—at the risk of losing its specificity. Above all, if Europe wants to preserve some relevance and the ability to influence the course of events in the new century, it will have to assert itself as an actor on the global, or at least regional, stage and therefore play by the rules governing the international system. Since it is unable to become a continental nation, the EU must project itself as a power endowed with strategic interests to defend, no longer as a mere doll's house in the vanguard of "global governance." No more than the United States, but for different reasons, can Europe allow itself any form of isolationism or naive idealism.

The evolution toward a strategic view of Europe began modestly with the adoption by the European Council in December 2003 of a "European security strategy," similar to the one published annually by the United States and with increasingly convergent content. This salutary exercise helped to reduce the initial gap between American and European geopolitical perceptions after September 11, opening the way to the improvement of transatlantic relations in recent years. Even better, the European Union made up for its internal paralysis—and for American weakening—by diplomatic activism which, in one form or another, placed Europeans in a leadership position in negotiations on the Iranian nuclear issue and the tensions between Lebanon and Syria.

This falling into step with the rest of the world does not mean that Europe must deny its values or give up its specific vocation in defining a new international order, quite the contrary. But, like the United States and the other major players in the international system, it needs to operate in two arenas: that of multilateralism, law, and the preservation of peace, of which it embodies the fullest realization, and that of power and interests, where it continues to appear as a sweet novice. Underlying the transatlantic dispute of 2003 regarding the principles of the international system—multilateralism against unilateralism, the status of the UN, the legitimacy of preemptive war—was the illusion that the European experience could be transposed to the governance of the planet. This meant disregarding what the extraordinary postwar European adventure owed to a specific historical experience, a cultural community, and a frozen strategic environment under American military protection. The question that now confronts Europe—as a political project but also as a continental bloc—is that of its capacity to avoid marginalization in the face of the dynamic relationship in progress between the United States and the new powers of Asia. This requires that the European Union preserve its existence and its specificity as a political project, which is now no longer guaranteed, and also adopt the diplomatic, military, and intellectual means to become a "global figure," short of being able to reach the rank of world power. In order to stay in the running, it must also respond to the economic and social challenges of weak growth, insufficient innovation, a nonexistent energy policy, deficient higher education and research, and a declining population.

Nothing of this can be accomplished without a reaction equivalent to a political refoundation of the European project, accompanied by a clear movement toward federalism at the institutional level, as is already the case in monetary, competition policy, and international trade matters: in these three areas Europe unquestionably exists on the world stage. But there are still no more visible signs of such a transformation than there is evidence of a new vision of American global leadership in Washington.[5] One may even legitimately wonder whether the combined effect of paralysis due to overextension and the ideological gap vis-à-vis global developments does not mean that the European enterprise missed its historical "window of opportunity" in the mid 1990s.

The circumstances of the early twenty-first century nevertheless provide European leaders with the new mobilizing theme that they have been seeking since Jacques Delors' "Single Market" project to replace peace and prosperity—however still relevant—as the new fundamental purpose of European unification: Europe must quite simply continue to exist and to weigh, that is, to defend its interests and its identity in the globalized world to come. Such a slogan has the virtues of being an obviously vital necessity and of being broad enough to mobilize all energies in all areas. Moreover, it stands in perfect continuity with the project of Europe's founding fathers, whose aim, beyond the historic reconciliation of France and Germany, was always to unite the resources of individual European nations in order to carry weight collectively on the international stage. Globalization, the emergence of new powers outside the Atlantic space, and the return of traditional geopolitics have only intensified this initial necessity. Europe will henceforth progress under the pressure of its external environment: it is past time for it to move to a grander scale and for a new generation of leaders to retrieve the vision necessary to inspire it with new energy.[6] Contrary to a common view, purposes, objectives, and challenges are not lacking, from competitiveness to foreign policy and defense, from energy policy to.immigration, not to mention higher education and research. European and world public opinion expects more from Europe, not less. All that is missing are the collective ambition of Europe's leaders and the resources to implement it.

5

THE WEAPONS OF PEACE

During the last two centuries the West's domination of world affairs went as far as to trigger global conflicts: the two world wars of the twentieth century were extensions of internal European rivalries. An indication that the world has changed is the fact that if a new world war were to erupt in the twenty-first century it would probably originate in Asia or the Middle East. But, as in the twentieth century, the preservation of democratic values and the stability of the world would require that the United States and the European Union be the victors of such a war. Even more important, the possibility of avoiding it also lies primarily in their hands.

DANGERS ON THE RISE

The risks threatening peace in the early years of this century are primarily geopolitical. They arise from three major developments: China's accession to world power status and the repercussions of that historic change in Asia and beyond, the stagnation of the Arab-Muslim world and internal rivalries in Islam for domination of the Middle East, and the competition between old and new powers for control of the energy resources indispensable for the acquisition or conservation of power itself. Increasing the danger posed by these three explosive problems, already bound together by the many interactions between globalization, energy, and Islamic fundamentalism, are the incendiary capacities of nuclear proliferation and terrorism.

The possibility that a regional or global conflict might begin in Asia does not necessarily require that Beijing have ambitions for dominance. All it would take would be a threat to the independence of Taiwan, guaranteed by the United States, a resurgence of Japanese militarism and Sino-Japanese tensions, exacerbated by China's rising power—which would also involve America—or an incident affecting the Korean peninsula, not to mention the historic rivalry between China and India or the reappearance of the cold war antagonism between Moscow and Beijing. Further west, a confrontation between the two regional nuclear powers, India and Pakistan, could not fail to have repercussions in the Middle East as well as East Asia and would again involve Washington, Beijing, and possibly Moscow. Peace in a heavily nuclearized region assailed by nationalism will depend on Chinese moderation, the quality of its relations with the United States, and American diplomatic skill.

Peace in the Middle East is threatened less by the Israeli-Palestinian conflict—however symbolic and tragic—and tensions between Islam and the West than by conflicts within the Arab-Muslim world and the regional ambitions of fundamentalist Iran—an energy power and potentially a nuclear one—with respect to the Persian Gulf and Iraq. The Iranian nuclear issue, the future of Iraq and Saudi Arabia and their indispensable oil reserves, the security of Israel, and a possible Islamist seizure of power in Egypt or elsewhere are all possible causes of regional, if not global, conflagration. For reasons having to do with history, geography, and energy, Europe would soon be involved alongside the United States. The Caucasus, Central Asia, and the Horn of Africa make up a third possible theater of crisis between energy-producing and energy-consuming powers—China, the United States, Russia, Iran—against a backdrop of ethnic and religious conflicts, whether local or regional. From Afghanistan to Somalia, Darfur, and Chad, the contagion of chaos and violence is penetrating dangerously into the heart of Africa.

The chances of avoiding war depend on the great powers' sense of responsibility, their collective ability to restrain nationalism, contain religious, ethnic, and territorial rivalries, and reduce tension between Islam and modernity, as well as on the success of the fight against nuclear proliferation and terrorism. Iran's entry into the nuclear club would engender a new arms race among its neighbors (Saudi Arabia, Egypt, Turkey) in an already explosive region of the world. According to the IAEA, approximately forty countries already have the technology required to produce a nuclear weapon.

On top of these increased strategic risks come truly global challenges, in the sense that they affect, directly or indirectly, all humanity: ecological threats associated with global warming, inadequate access to water, malnutrition, new pandemics. Until now, these scourges have been approached primarily in humanitarian terms, but that is no longer the case since their impact on the most prosperous nations and the stability of the world has become clear. Beyond the ecological aspect, the challenges of global warming are now inseparable from economic growth, development, and the question of energy supplies. Similarly, poverty and inequality, combined with population increases in developing countries, foster civil wars, mass migration, ethnic conflict, failed states, terrorism, and the spread of weapons of mass destruction. Environmental and humanitarian challenges have thus also become explosive geopolitical challenges.

Global warming is a long-term trend that can be attenuated but not eliminated, particularly because the developed countries' efforts to reduce pollution will be more than offset by the growth in energy consumption in developing countries, notably China and India. According to the World Bank, the emission of greenhouse gases, whose dissipation in the atmosphere takes several decades, will increase on the order of 50 percent between now and 2030 and could double by 2050, because of anticipated increases in energy consumption.[1] The latest UN estimates consequently predict an increase in the world's mean temperature of between 2 and 4.5 degrees centigrade between now and 2100.

The harmful effects of global warming are many, particularly in developing countries: environmental change, deforestation and desertification, pollution and unhealthy cities, conflicts over water supplies, and declining ability to maintain public health and food security. Climate change thereby aggravates other worldwide evils: new pandemics (SARS, bird flu, AIDS) with devastating effects on the life expectancy and economic activity of the populations of sub-Saharan Africa; malnutrition for 815 million people, despite the increase in world food supplies; and lack of potable water for a billion of them, the cause of 25,000 deaths every day, half of them children.

While the African continent has finally started to benefit from the great winds of globalization and reform, away from the pitiful view commonly held of it in Europe, it remains the primary victim of these scourges, and the situation, particularly south of the Sahara, has continued to deteriorate. African economic growth, at 5.8 percent in 2006 and estimated at 5.5 percent in 2007, has reached these levels largely because those countries that export oil and other raw materials have profited from soaring prices. Many others are confronting dramatic problems: humanitarian tragedy in Darfur, an unprecedented economic crisis in Zimbabwe, floods, critical food situations in many regions of East, West, and South Africa, and conflicts and political disturbances in Ethiopia, the Ivory Coast, and the eastern part of the Democratic Republic of the Congo and the rich oil-producing region of the Niger delta. Hence, only six countries, most of them in North Africa, will probably reach the chief millennium development goal of reducing by half the portion of the population living on less than one dollar a day.

THE NARROW PATH OF WESTERN SOLIDARITY

This rise of instability all around the Atlantic space should, as a first step, lead to a defensive strengthening of Western solidarity, based on shared challenges, interests, and values and the need to combine the economic, demographic, diplomatic, and military capacities of the United Sates and Europe to respond to it, including to be in a stronger position in the future to engage China and India.

The necessities of the fight against terrorism, nuclear proliferation, and organized cross-border crime have already led the European Union and the United States to deepen transatlantic legal cooperation, overcoming sensitivities about sovereignty even within Europe. The two sides of the Atlantic are also facing increasingly similar and complex political and humanitarian challenges in the area of immigration, which has given rise to a new form of cooperation in an attempt to provide solutions that are acceptable from both the political and the humanitarian standpoint. The UN estimates that international migratory movements now involve nearly 200 million people—a record in human history—and continue to grow despite the stiffening of national controls. Forty percent of these migrants end up in Europe or the United States, coming from Africa, Latin America, and Asia, and, thanks to high fertility rates, they represent a growing proportion of the younger generation in Europe and the United States.[2] In the United States, estimates of the number of illegal immigrants range from 11 to 20 million, compared to 11 million in the country legally. Europe has regularized the status of about 20 million people, but estimates of the number of illegals—3 million in 1998 is the latest official figure—have been made very difficult by the elimination of border controls within the European Union. Traditionally more welcoming than Europe, the United States now shares Europe's fears about the preservation of national values and national identity as well as concerns about security and terrorism. As for the European Union, overwhelmed by the wave of immigrants from Africa and from its eastern borders and confronted with the failure of its traditional model of integration, it has been considering the American experience with less condescension than previously. On both sides of the Atlantic help in the economic development of countries that are the source of immigrants seems indispensable to reduce the pressure, but the contribution of the immigrant workforce is equally important for domestic growth in light of the aging population, especially in Europe.

In the economic sphere, the transatlantic dimension is already pre-dominant, to the point of challenging the relevance of the European Single Market.[3] Rather than seeking to turn themselves into "European champions," many multinational enterprises on the continent have formed alliances or merged with their American counterparts to in-crease their presence in the United States and to create companies with global reach—Vivendi Universal, DaimlerChrysler, Alcatel-Lucent, and many others—with variable success. The prospect of hostile takeovers of enterprises, or even entire industrial sectors, deemed strategic by companies or investment funds from emerging countries, themselves often controlled by less than reliable states or individuals, has become a common concern on both sides of the Atlantic. Long more sensitive to the strategic dimension of economic affairs, the United States is much better equipped in this area than the European Union and its member states, which lack a legal mechanism to oppose an unwanted takeover bid in areas affecting national or European security or independence, such as energy, health, finance, or telecommunications. The European Commission still considers this concern heretical in the name of free capital movements and the principles of an open globalized economy. This amounts, however, to a disregard of the geopolitical changes brought about by globalization and the existence of explicit or oblique mechanisms for controlling foreign investments in strategic sectors of most great economic powers, from the Exon-Florio legislation in the United States to the recent Chinese law on foreign investments. It would, of course, be preferable if a mechanism of this kind were put in place at the EU level to maintain the cohesion of the Single Market, but this presupposes that the prospect of a political Europe remains alive. In the meantime, Brussels should grant the member states more leeway to control, within reasonable limits, bids to acquire strategic companies by investors outside the EU.

Growing competition from the huge Asian economy should also encourage Europe and the United States to better structure the transat-lantic economy at the institutional and regulatory levels so as to solidify its primacy and homogeneity. The often discussed formal establishment of a transatlantic free trade zone, which already exists de facto, seems less relevant in this regard than the harmonization of standards and the integration of financial markets. The largest initial public offering in history was conducted in the Hong Kong and Shanghai markets in October 2006, when shares of the Chinese bank ICBC were sold for 22 billion dollars. In this context, the merger of Euronext and the New York Stock Exchange takes on particular significance. Going forward, after the liberalization of air traffic, shared concerns about energy security might encourage the Atlantic partners to pool their supplies in case of crisis. And so on.

Finally and most important, in political and moral terms, the United States and Europe are, each in its own way, "sentinels of liberty": the chief protectors of democracy in the world and of the preservation of an international system based on law and tolerance in the service of humanistic values. The nations and political communities that carry those values will be ever more in the minority, demographically, in number, and in power, in the multipolar world to come. Furthermore, the promotion of formal democracy superficially embodied by "free" elections may—at least temporarily—turn against democratic values themselves, as occurred in Germany between the two world wars and is now happening in some parts of the Arab-Muslim world.

These risks clearly illustrate the limitations, indeed the dangers, of a purely defensive Western solidarity in the face of the rest of the world. This attitude first carries the risk of fostering the emergence of a new confrontation between North and South, which the "anti-imperialist" alliance of Latin American nationalists and radical Islamists, with Beijing's blessing, is already endeavoring to provoke by exploiting the recent setbacks suffered by American foreign policy: by way of illustration, two of the three most prominent guests at the African Union summit of 2006 were Venezuelan president Chávez and his Iranian counterpart Ahmadinejad. In a more positive spirit, it is entirely natural that the diplomacy of large emerging countries such as India and Brazil be increasingly organized around a certain solidarity of the developing world in its effort to catch up historically with the industrialized countries in the WTO and other multilateral forums.

Furthermore, whatever the power maintained by the West, an exclusively defensive attitude would, because of the numerical and demographic superiority of the rest of the planet, immediately place the Western democracies in a bunker from which Western civilization and the world would have little hope of benefiting. Closing borders to immigrant populations in search of survival, excluding, except under exceptional circumstances, emerging country multinationals from control of Western companies, and preventive overarming and obsessive security measures go against the principles and values that define the civilization of the Enlightenment and have ensured its preeminence in the modern era. To ward off the ghost of the clash of civilizations, the democratic West will therefore have to continue to foster, to the greatest possible degree, the openness, fluidity, and solidarity of the world in the service of universal humanistic values, with the defensive strengthening of the Atlantic bound operating solely in support of that goal and as an ultimate safeguard in case of failure. This, in no way, means that the democratic agenda promoted by the United States, in keeping with a long historical and diplomatic tradition, as well as by the European Union in the framework of its enlargement policy should be abandoned. Belonging or not belonging to Western civilization or the democratic community cannot, however, serve as the ultimate division in international society: the real split is that between moderates and extremists, tolerance and terrorism, civilization and barbarism among states as within civil societies.

This dual strategy, a narrow path between defensive solidarity and openness to the world, is all the more indispensable on the part of the West that only a renewed partnership between Europe and America can defuse the time bombs darkening the future and threatening peace: the proliferation of areas in chaos, the erosion of multilateralism by globalization, the fundamentalist isolation of large parts of the Arab-Muslim world, and global ecological and humanitarian challenges. The West retains an advantage of timing, as these problems must be addressed in the course of the next two decades, that is, while the Western world still holds its lead over the rest of the planet in terms of economic wealth, financial power, diplomatic influence, institutional experience, and scientific and technological expertise. This historical advantage provides it with the responsibility, and the opportunity, to take the initiative to reorganize the world according to the values of peace, freedom, openness, democracy, and progress that are its defining characteristics. In that way, by resolutely following this path to the benefit of the common good, the United States and Europe will recover the legitimacy and prestige necessary to the preservation of their leadership.

This enterprise can indeed succeed only with the cooperation of the entire international community, but its different components are not at all in equal positions to undertake the task. The least advanced countries of Africa and Asia are the principal victims of disorder around the world and cannot do much about it, except to improve, with the help of international organizations, their political and economic governance so that their populations can effectively benefit from the fruits of globalization and aid from rich countries. The emerging countries, particularly the future great economic powers, China, India, Russia, and Brazil, have an indispensable role to play in the organization of a new international order, in particular in the areas of environmental preservation and development assistance, but they cannot be expected to take the lead. They are by definition in a phase of economic and political catching up with the old industrialized countries and will for long remain unsettling elements in the existing international system. They must in addition confront, on a continental scale, the humanitarian, social, and environmental challenges threatening the planet and legitimately argue that the West has no grounds for restraining their development to resolve problems largely inherited from its industrialization and domination over the last fifteen decades. It is all the more difficult to counter the argument in the name of global solidarity and responsibility as the economic growth of China and India is improving the condition of hundreds of millions of individuals, whereas the United States and Europe are far from doing what is necessary to remedy global warming and the nutritional and sanitary problems of the poorest. Geopolitically, moreover, China and Russia have every interest in playing their own tune to assert their power in the face of the Western camp. The indispensable contribution of emerging countries to the preservation of the world's public goods and to the reconstruction of an international order can therefore only result from a pressure and exemplarity that the democratic West is today alone in a position to provide.

THREE PRIORITIES FOR THE NEXT TWO DECADES

The first item on the transatlantic agenda for the next two decades must be the adaptation of the international system to the new situation arising from globalization and the radicalization of conflict, before these two tidal waves completely wash away the positive legacy of the last sixty years. The advent of a multipolar world that is fragmented and dangerous requires more than ever the restoration of a legitimate and effective multilateral system, the keystone of which remains the United Nations. The missions of international institutions must be refocused on the new global challenges, and their governance reformed, to better reflect the worldwide nature and interdependence of problems as well as the economic and political rise of emerging countries, while at the same time ensuring that such opening does not paralyze or distort these institutions.

Proposed changes in the membership of the UN Security Council that have been fruitlessly discussed for years clearly illustrate the difficulty of the process. The emerging and developing countries that make up a large majority of the international community criticize the great powers for monopolizing the Security Council, and they use the General Assembly as a negative counterweight, which undermines the credibility of the multilateral system's leading institution. The number of permanent members of the Security Council with veto power—the five victors of the Second World War—could not be increased without risking paralysis, especially as Russia and China, two emerging powers that in fact represent ideological currents and interests opposed to those of the West, already belong to that club. On the other hand, the admission of new permanent members without veto power and the reform of the system of nonpermanent members should consecrate the new international responsibilities of nations such as Germany, Japan, India, Brazil, and South Africa. As a general rule, accession to leadership positions in the UN's institutional framework should be strictly conditioned to fully responsible behavior in conformity with the charter, as provided in its article 23 with regard to admission to the Security Council. The candidacy of Venezuela under Chávez for nonpermanent membership on the Security Council and the participation of countries that routinely abuse human rights on commissions supposed to protect them obviously contradict this principle and affect the credibility of the entire system. The UN Charter must also be able to confront new disorders: mass terrorism and nuclear proliferation, which raise the question of preventive war, and ethnic cleansing and genocide, which call for a right of humanitarian intervention against offending states.

The necessary strengthening of the effectiveness and credibility of the UN system must also involve the organizations that deal with the major world problems of the day—nuclear proliferation (IAEA), public health (WHO), food and water (FAO)—to which should be added new institutions dedicated to energy and the environment. The entire architecture of these institutions and the system of world governance as a whole need to be reconsidered. Having proliferated for more than fifty years, specialized agencies now overlap and thereby engender high coordination costs. To take a single example, three agencies based in Rome are now concerned with food security: the FAO, the World Food Program (WFP), and the International Fund for Agricultural Development (IFAD). On the other hand, there is no institution devoted to the protection of one of the principal public resources of the planet, the environment. The establishment of a world environment organization, as has frequently been contemplated, would represent a major advance, provided those involved recognize the inefficiencies produced by a fragmented system whose overall architecture needs rethinking.

In the economic sphere the successful conclusion of the Doha round of trade negotiations—on which depend growth and development around the world in the next few decades—and the introduction of qualified majority voting in the decision-making processes of the WTO constitute the main priorities, followed by the adaptation of the traditional missions of the IMF—begun in Singapore in September 2006—and the World Bank to the changes in the international monetary, financial, and economic systems.

More broadly, globalization and the increasingly global nature of tomorrow's challenges call for a shift of the multilateral system toward more effective forms of governance. Most large international organizations today are still governed by the canons of classic international law, invented in the sixteenth century and based on the absolute sovereignty of states and their equality within the "concert of nations." They therefore obey an essentially intergovernmental logic, whose inefficiencies have been demonstrated in the context of the unification of Europe, driven by a mixed system of governance that includes a strong dose of federalism. And what is true for 15 or 27 nations is even truer for institutions with 150 or 200 member states such as the WTO and the UN. While the institutional forms of integrated governance that produced the construction of Europe are not immediately transferable to worldwide organizations, this is clearly the direction to follow, first with respect to regional organizations such as Mercosur, the African Union, and ASEAN and then for the entire multilateral system. This requires that the emerging and developing countries, whose influence in international organizations will continue to grow, exhibit a sense of responsibility, as the perpetuation of antagonism between North and South can only lead in the long term to the decline of multilateralism.

The second imperative for the next few decades is unquestionably the integration of the Arab-Muslim world into economic and political modernity, that is, into globalization and the culture of democracy. The duplicitous motives invoked by the Bush administration to justify the war in Iraq and the ensuing chaos have unfortunately discredited the American agenda of "democratization" in the Middle East. It nonetheless remains true that, whatever form it may take, the participation of the Arab-Muslim world in the benefits of globalization and political freedom is an imperative for world stability and the best long-term response to the rise of radical Islamism. There are many mutually reinforcing reasons for this: attacking the economic, social, and political roots of terrorism, the need to soothe the growing antagonism between the West and a Muslim world comprising about 1.2 billion people, almost the equivalent of the population of China, guaranteeing energy supplies indispensable for the world economy, the need to reduce explosive tensions within the region, between Israel and those who remain intent on its destruction, but also between Shiites and Sunnis, radical and moderate Muslims, and rival ambitions for regional power. Let's just imagine the consequences of a seizure of power by Islamist parties in nuclearized and terrorism-infiltrated Pakistan or in Saudi Arabia, with the largest oil reserves on the planet.

In recent years developments in Iraq, Iran, Palestine, and Egypt have, however, demonstrated that the elimination by force of dictatorial regimes and the holding of "free" elections were far from enough to institute democracy, favoring, on the contrary, fundamentalist political parties and ethnic and religious rivalries. Subject to much criticism in Europe and in the region, the American vision of a "greater democratic Middle East" has been discredited by the Iraqi fiasco, its favorable consequences for Iran, and Washington's abdication in the face of the deterioration of the Israeli-Palestinian conflict. But Europe unfortunately has done nothing to remedy American shortcomings. The European approach to the modernization of the Arab-Muslim world is set in the framework of its recent "neighborhood policy," inaugurated in May 2004 to coincide with the admission of ten new member states from Central and Eastern and Europe. This policy is aimed at stabilizing the states located on the eastern and southern borders of the enlarged Union (notably North Africa and the Middle East) through aid and cooperation programs conditioned on the implementation of political, economic, and legal reforms by the countries concerned. Ten years earlier, in 1995, the EU inaugurated the so-called Barcelona Process aimed at creating a Euro-Mediterranean community based on economic, political, and cultural cooperation.

This administrative approach to the modernization of the most Westernized portion of the Arab-Muslim world has not produced the anticipated results. It has been criticized, in particular, for its excessively technocratic nature, a certain laxity in the enforcement of the conditions for providing aid, the weakness of incentives for reform, and, most important, the lack of organized support for local reform movements.[4] In the end, however controversial the beginning of its implementation, the American vision of an economic and political liberalization of the Arab-Muslim world remains more relevant and mobilizing than the patchwork of small bureaucratic steps taken by Europe to date.

For whoever was familiar with Lebanon, Turkey, or Tunisia in the 1950s and 1960s, the contemporary debate about the "compatibility" of Islam with modernity and democracy has no basis in reality. Compared to that period, epitomized by the secular modernizing nationalism of Habib Bourguiba, it is clear that the Arab-Muslim world has regressed politically, economically, and socially under the combined influence of authoritarian and corrupt regimes, the population explosion, and its inability to profit from economic globalization, despite its staggering oil wealth. Fundamentalist movements have merely profited from this failure for political and religious purposes, by alleviating poverty and injustice and by exploiting resentment against Israel, America, and Western modernity as a whole.

Putting a halt to this regressive movement would require that the disastrous choice between defense of the status quo and the progress of Islamism be overcome. The third way that is necessary is that of active and organized support for moderate and reformist parties and movements in the civil society of each of the countries concerned, accompanied by a program of development assistance comparable to the Marshall Plan, strictly conditioned on the implementation of political and economic reform. This support must in turn be backed by the indispensable active commitment of the political, economic, and intellectual elite of moderate Islam against the Islamist ideological war machine. The success of a program of this kind, however, presupposes that the United States and Europe recover their credibility and prestige in the region by helping restore peace and stability in Iraq, the Middle East, and Afghanistan and by containing Iranian ambitions.

Yet, while the economic and social dimensions are essential to explain the rise of fundamentalism, it would be mistaken to underestimate the search for identity involved in the religious revival in the Islamic world. This revival participates in a deep-rooted movement toward self-reappropriation and a quest for meaning at work in every latitude and in every religion, including the United States and secularized Europe, with which it will be necessary to come to terms. Here, as elsewhere, the dividing line lies between moderates and extremists, Islam and Islamism, not between Islam and democracy. The promotion of the role of women in society, the defense of the principle of secularism, and education lie at the heart of this battle.

The third major priority concerns the preservation of the world's public goods and the rescue of sub-Saharan Africa, a continent staggering under the perverse interaction of environmental, health, and nutritional disasters and whose per capita revenue has increased by only 0.3 of 1 percent since 1964.[5] On each of the eight millennium development goals defined by the UN to be reached by 2015—ranging from the reduction by half of extreme poverty to primary education for all, and including a halt to the spread of AIDS and the promotion of women's equality and autonomy—indicators for the majority of African countries show the enormous distance that remains to be traveled. According to the economist Jeffrey Sachs, in order to reach these goals, the rich countries would have had to inject 121 billion dollars by 2006 to supplement the efforts of the developing countries of the South, with that figure rising to 185 billion by 2015, that is, 0.54 percent of their GDP as opposed to today's 0.25 percent.

From the work of international organizations on these various scourges, however, some useful lessons can be derived to mobilize the international community and assist it in acting intelligently. The first concerns the interdependence between the issues of growth and development, energy, the environment, and global humanitarian challenges as well as the existing de facto solidarity, in the shorter or longer term, between the developed countries, the emerging world, and the poorest countries in the face of these challenges. We have already seen how growth increases the demand for and consumption of energy, with a twofold negative impact on the ecological and geopolitical equilibrium of the world, and delayed effects to the detriment of the most deprived populations on the planet. Another example of the connection between growth, the environment, and geopolitics is the fact that the search for clean energy favors a revival of civilian nuclear power, including in emerging countries, with the associated risks of a deviation toward military uses.

A second lesson to be learned is that there is no choice to be made between economic development and preservation of the environment or public health, because their deterioration has a high measurable economic cost. It is one of the notable virtues of the Stern Report, published in the fall of 2006, to have made this relationship explicit, thereby transforming ecological concern into an economic policy choice.[6] According to the report, a temperature increase of from 5 to 6 degrees centigrade—a real possibility in the course of the twenty-first century—could result in an average decline of 5 to 10 percent of world GDP, a decline that might exceed 10 percent for the poorest countries. At the present time pollution and environmental degradation resulting from unregulated industrialization are already costing China about 10 percent of its GDP. In contrast, the cost of a serious program for reducing emissions of greenhouse gases would amount to only 1 percent of world GDP between now and 2050. Hence not only is the fight against global warming compatible with economic development, but that fight is of obvious economic benefit. Similar reasoning can be applied to other humanitarian challenges, even if the economic cost of abstention in matters of health or nutrition has a less direct effect on rich and emerging countries than on sub-Saharan Africa and the poorest Asian countries. AIDS, for example, is devastating a significant portion of the active farming population of sub-Saharan Africa, which has further worsened malnutrition.

The third lesson is perhaps the most important one: the remedies for each one of these global challenges are not out of reach. They have in common the fact that they often depend on technological innovation and require relatively modest financial resources in the scale of things in the world economy. The solutions with respect to the environment generally consist of reducing the dependence of economic growth on fossil fuels. To accomplish this, Europe chose the multilateralist path of the Kyoto Protocol, based on a reduction of CO_2 emissions and the establishment of a carbon trading market. But its investments in clean energy sources are still inadequate. The United States, which did not ratify the Kyoto Protocol, thought to impose too many constraints on growth, has moved closer to it recently on the regional and local levels and, most important, has implemented a national program of incentives for technological innovation in clean energy, which appears to have reconciled the two imperatives of ecology and development. It has made massive investments in nuclear energy, for example, in battery-powered vehicles, and in other new energy sources. The transition to an economy with a low level of carbon dioxide emissions in the rich countries and the rapid transfer of technologies increasing energy efficiency to emerging countries—from which half the CO_2 emissions will come by 2050—appear to be the two pillars of the fight against global warming and its consequences. In the end, the ecological future of the planet will probably depend on a Chinese-American "new deal" consisting of self-limitation and technological cooperation on energy and the environment

With respect to health, solutions depend on improvements in the nutritional situation and in access to potable water and generic drugs

in the poorest countries, but equally on the struggle against a short-
age of qualified health workers, which has had acute effects in sixty of
the most deprived countries. Similarly, with regard to nutrition, experts
agree that "the world can feed the world." Despite the deterioration of
soils and an annual average increase of 70 million in the world population up to 2025, global food security should not be threatened.[7] Solutions to the chronic malnutrition of 815 million people once again involve technological innovation (improvement of plant species through
genetic engineering, particularly GMOs, recourse to sustainable development methods) and a better division of world agricultural production. The fierce agricultural competition between Europe and the
United States in developing countries increases the food dependency of
those countries on world markets at the very time when increased Chinese demand threatens to corner too much of the international grain
market, already resulting in higher prices for food products.

TOWARD A NEW ATLANTIC PACT

These observations converge in a general conclusion: the resolution of
the great challenges of the twenty-first century is primarily a question
of political will, made more difficult by the global nature of both problems and solutions. In the absence of genuine world governance, that
political will has to be expressed through international cooperation and
international organizations, and its implementation should mobilize all
available forces: developed and emerging countries, national and local
actors, NGOs, the private and nonprofit sectors, all acting within the
framework of a general plan. Since the United States and Europe generally hold the keys to the relevant agricultural, technological, pharma-
ceutical, financial, and political sets of issues, it is up to them to take the
initiative in this global new deal, which they should negotiate with the
major emerging countries for the common good.

The capacity of the two principal centers of the Western world
together to stimulate the international cooperation required depends,
in the first place, on their success in undertaking necessary reforms in

their own economic and social systems. Like the developing countries indebted to the IMF in the 1980s and 1990s, and more successfully, it is hoped, Europe and the United States must subject themselves to a genuine program of structural adjustment to globalization. Among domestic reforms, priority should be given to the reduction of overall energy consumption, particularly in the United States, and of dependence on imported fossil fuel, imperative for both ecological and geopolitical reasons. Next comes the liberalization of global agricultural trade, in which the excessive protectionism of Europe and the United States has blocked completion of the Doha round, thereby limiting access by Western economies to the market in services in emerging countries. Immediately following in the list of priorities come structural reforms of economic and social systems with a view to confronting competition from emerging countries without recourse to massive protectionism. Particular targets in this area are, in the United States, the low rate of household savings and the economic structure of the social safety net and, in Europe, reform of the tax, labor, and higher educational systems that hold back competitiveness and growth.

Without these structural reforms, democratic pressure within Western societies weakened by globalization will sooner or later lead to protectionism and populism, and, as the economic and social position of the least-favored classes deteriorates, to increasing antagonism toward China and even India, which would be detrimental to economic growth and to peace. Sinophobia has already made inroads in the United States, particularly among Democratic voters, as the trade deficit with China has grown. Conversely, the implementation of this structural adjustment program in the Atlantic world would place Europe and America in a position of strength for negotiations with Beijing (and soon New Delhi) on a general agreement on energy, the environment, monetary policy, and the restoration of a balanced trade.

Similarly, in the geopolitical realm, the United States and Europe should first work together to stabilize Afghanistan and Iraq and contain Iranian ambitions, a necessary condition for their credibility and for international security. There is consensus on this necessity with respect to Afghanistan and Iran, but the transatlantic rifts that accompanied the American-led invasion of Iraq and the resulting fiasco have prevented a similar consensus from developing about Iraq. Yet an American withdrawal from Iraq under the present circumstances would constitute a serious failure for the entire Western community vis-à-vis the Arab-Muslim world and would create a more dangerous situation in the heart of the Middle East than the Afghanistan of the Taliban in 2001. A premature withdrawal of coalition forces would run the risk of intensifying the civil war between the Sunni, Shiite, and Kurdish communities and accelerating the dissolution of the state to the benefit of Iran's regional ambitions and the aims of al Qaeda. Increasing political pressure for disengagement in the United States should consequently encourage the Europeans and the entire international community to mobilize rapidly to help stabilize Iraq in the common interest.

In the longer term, the two major centers of the Western world must set themselves to the task of reestablishing the Atlantic partnership on a basis of burden sharing and mutual recognition. Geopolitical developments in recent years have generally demonstrated the reality of this complementarity of the United States and the European Union. In strategic and military matters Europe has neither the means nor the real ambition to do without American superiority, which thus remains the guaranty of the preservation of Western interests in the broad sense and of world stability in the framework of NATO and within ad hoc coalitions. The transatlantic compromise reached at the Riga summit in December 2006 extended NATO's capacity to intervene beyond its traditional borders with the cooperation of external partners, such as Japan, Australia, and South Korea, on demand and depending on immediate needs. The EU must nonetheless continue to develop its own military intervention capabilities in its immediate neighborhood and help to stabilize centers of tension beyond, as it is doing in Afghanistan, Lebanon, the Balkans, and Africa.

With regard to soft power, on the other hand, the loss by the United States of credibility, legitimacy, and room for diplomatic maneuver offers Europe the opportunity to enhance the status of its own resources and demonstrate its usefulness on the international stage, as it has done in the last few years in negotiations on the Iranian nuclear matter. In Afghanistan, for example, the stabilization of the country in the face of the Taliban's comeback requires political, economic, and social steps to complement military action on the ground, where Europe already has a significant presence. Synergies between Europe and America are also evident in their respective degrees of knowledge of different geopolitical and cultural environments: more familiar with Asia than the Europeans, the Americans would have every interest in operating in close cooperation with Europe in the Arab-Muslim world, on the eastern borders of the European Union, and even in Latin America. A division of labor along these lines will, however, fail to eliminate the cartoonish contrast between Mars and Venus popularized by Robert Kagan a few years ago if Europe does not increase the current level of its strategic and diplomatic contributions, particularly in the Middle East.[8] Similarly, European strengths cannot excuse the United States, in the general interest, from the task of restoring its international credit, particularly in the Islamic world.

Reestablishing the Atlantic community on new foundations requires more than deriving benefit from these synergies within an institution-alized strategic partnership: it involves a genuine mutual recognition of the contribution of each one by the other. The Europeans must accept their strategic dependence on the United States and their solidar-ity with Washington in the Atlantic alliance and the Western commu-nity. That does not in any way preclude criticism and disagreement, nor does it authorize the European Union—or its national leaders—to define itself on the international stage as a counterweight to American power. In return, America must recognize at their true value the con-tributions of the European Union to the progress of peace, democracy, and prosperity internally and on its borders, and to the management of international crises, as well as its role as a model of governance and regional integration for large segments of the international commu-nity. The expansion of Europe to the south and then to the east of the original Community of Six and its power of attraction at the gates of

Asia have represented a remarkable tool for lastingly replacing dictatorship and underdevelopment with democracy, the rule of law, and the market economy and hence with peace and prosperity over most of the European continent.

The United States, to be sure, has always championed the policy of enlarging the European Union, which it rightly considers one of the Union's major accomplishments. But it has not granted Europe all the political credit due to it, in the transatlantic strategic dialogue, from this contribution to the stability of an essential part of Eurasia. Further, Washington continues to advocate the expansion of Europe to Turkey, and beyond, without giving appropriate consideration to the negative impact of this unlimited expansion on the effectiveness and attractive power of the European enterprise in the eyes of its own citizens.

In this regard, Europe is now confronting a very serious dilemma. Further enlargement is neither desirable nor possible in the current state of institutional affairs and democratic opposition. At the same time, European techniques for modernization, stabilization, and democratization that have proved themselves in the context of enlargement are more necessary than ever in the large southern and eastern regions bordering the Union. Unless European unification regains strength by moving toward further integration or, conversely, loosens into a mere international organization, further enlargement appears unlikely in the foreseeable future. The EU's external policy must therefore focus on reformed versions of its neighborhood policy, such as strategic partnerships and other institutional forms lying somewhere between association and full membership that need to be as attractive as membership for the countries concerned.

To succeed in this difficult diplomatic exercise, Europe will need all the political support and recognition it is entitled to expect from Washington. At a time when the Iraqi fiasco, on one side of the Atlantic, and the rejection of enlargement, on the other, risk causing the United States and Europe to turn inward, both have to cooperate and find new ways to continue promoting democratic values in the years to come.

CONCLUSION

SHAPING THE WORLD TO COME

Since I began writing this book in the summer of 2006, some of the changes I intended to underscore and tie together have accelerated dramatically, with the beneficial side effect of intensifying public awareness of our entry into a new, not so flat world.

The international financial turmoil and domestic recession resulting from the U.S. subprime crisis have turned the page of twenty years of financial deregulation and unrestrained market "creativity." These developments, of yet uncertain consequence, are furthering both the shift of global economic power from West to East and the return of governments onto the world's economic stage.

The continuous rise of food prices caused largely by increased consumption in China and India is threatening the poorest populations of Africa and Asia while contributing to the return of inflation in the West.

Amidst ever more alarming expert reports, climate change has become the primary focus of world public opinion and now dominates the agenda of most governments and international organizations. From a different standpoint, record-high oil prices have also stressed the strategic role of energy in redesigning the economic balance of power and the geopolitics of the twenty-first century.

What I have called the emerging world revolution has become a daily reality, as China, India, Russia, the Gulf states and many other former "developing countries" increasingly assert themselves on the global stage, making inroads in the West in multiple ways, from business and finance to diplomacy, from energy to information and culture. Spectacularly, in the last two months of 2007 alone, sovereign wealth funds from China, Singapore, Abu Dhabi, and other emerging nations injected some thirty billion dollars into Western (primarily American) financial powerhouses hit by the fallout from the U.S. subprime crisis in exchange for significant minority stakes in their equity. China is already the second world economy in terms of purchasing power. And this is just the beginning: non-Western powers will have an increasing influence on virtually every aspect of world affairs and, eventually, on the domestic affairs of the Western world.

This acceleration of globalization, in the broader meaning developed in this book, confronts the West with a twofold challenge: trying to shape the world to come, short of being able to continue mastering it, while learning to share global power with other, non-Western, sometimes nondemocratic, often imperial nations.

Power sharing will be a far more difficult learning process for the United States, as the former sole global superpower, than for the European Union, a quintessential soft power that has made shared sovereignty and multilateral governance defining features of its internal and external relations. Leading in a multipolar world has far-reaching implications for future United States foreign policy, its attitude toward multilateralism, international institutions, and key global issues such as climate change and economic development as well as the restoration of its international soft power.

The ability of the West to shape tomorrow's world is contingent on both the state of transatlantic solidarity and the leadership capacity of the United States and the European Union. As anticipated, transatlantic relations have improved significantly since the change of leadership in Germany and France, where calls for a long-term closer Euro-American economic and strategic relationship have recently multiplied. The rise

of the emerging world to global power status is likely to spur America and Europe toward greater unity, hopefully without causing them to fall into the trap of a "West against the rest" attitude.

Yet, the United States and Europe each face a different set of internal challenges that may work against this renewed sense of solidarity. Furthermore, the ability to exercise effective leadership together on the world stage, or simply to react to the rise to power of emerging giants, requires each to overcome its current political immobility. While in a far better position than Europe to do so, America must cease to focus on the "war on terror," the Iraq fiasco, and idiosyncratic moral and religious debates as the cornerstones of both its domestic politics and foreign policies in order to more broadly embrace twenty-first-century geopolitics and produce political leaders of the stature called for by the challenges ahead. Change at the top must bring the United States closer to the rest of the world and its global responsibilities, not further distance American politics and society from the international community.

Europe, for its part, must at last decide whether or not it wants to remain relevant—politically and even economically—in tomorrow's world and, if so, take the necessary steps to become a true global player. It has no more than the next decade to do so.

For all their democratic shortcomings, China's and even Russia's ruling classes have demonstrated strategic vision and the leadership skills to bring about change and use globalization to restore national power, leadership that, unfortunately, seem in short supply in the West.

The long-run superiority of democratic government over authoritarian regimes to produce stable, egalitarian, and robust societies does not eliminate the need for political vision and courage, intelligent leadership, hard work, and moral standing in this part of the world. Far from it.

NOTES

PREFACE

1. See, in particular, the report by the Human Security Center of Vancouver, *Human Security Report 2005: War and Peace in the Twenty-first Century* (New York: Oxford University Press, 2006).

INTRODUCTION

1. Thomas L. Friedman, *The World Is Flat: A Brief History of the Twenty-first Century* (New York: Farrar, Straus and Giroux, 2005).

1. THE NEW FACE OF GLOBALIZATION

1. Angus Maddison, "The World Economy: A Millennial Perspective" (Paris: OECD, 2006).

2. See, for example, Ali Laïdi, *Retour de flamme: Comment la mondialisation a accouché du terrorisme* (Paris: Calmann-Lévy, 2006). Another connection between globalization and terrorism, of course, has to do with the use terrorist networks make of the technological, financial, and logistical opportunities that globalization offers along with widespread freedom of movement.

3. See, for example, Gilles Kepel, *Jihad: The Trail of Political Islam*, trans. Anthony F. Roberts (Cambridge: Harvard University Press, 2002); and Antoine Babsous, *L'islamisme, une révolution avortée?* (Paris: Hachette, 2000).

4. Dominic Wilson and Roopa Purushothaman, "Dreaming with the BRICs: The Path to 2050," Global Economic Paper no. 99 (New York: Goldman Sachs, 2003).

5. As of 2006, China had a middle class of 150 million and 5 to 10 million people with purchasing power equivalent to that of wealthy classes in Western countries.

2. THE END OF THE ATLANTIC ERA

1. For a rebuttal, the reader may refer to chapter 6 of my book, *An Alliance at Risk: The United States and Europe Since September 11*, trans. George Holoch (Baltimore: Johns Hopkins University Press, 2003); and, from a different perspective, to Thierry Chopin, *L'Amérique et l'Europe: La dérive des continents?* (Paris: Grasset, 2006).

2. For an analysis of the current European crisis, see my essay "The End of Europe?" *Foreign Affairs* 84.6 (November/December 2005).

3. *Science, Technology and Industry: OECD Perspectives 2006* (Paris: OECD, December 2006).

4. Richard B. Freeman, *Does Globalization of the Scientific/Engineering Workforce Threaten U.S. Economic Leadership?* NBER Working Paper no. 11457 (Cambridge: National Bureau of Economic Research, July 2005).

3. THE GEOPOLITICS OF GLOBALIZATION

1. Francis Fukuyama, *The End of History and the Last Man* (New York: Free, 1992).

2. Samuel Huntington, *The Clash of Civilizations and the Remaking of World Order* (New York: Simon and Schuster, 1996).

3. On the Iranian threat, see Thérèse Delpech, *Le Grand perturbateur: Réflexions sur la question iraninienne* (Paris: Grasset, 2007).

4. For a Chinese viewpoint on the geopolitical implications of its rise, see the series of articles titled "China Rising" in *Foreign Affairs* 84.5 (September-October 2005). For an American assessment, see CSIS/Peterson Institute for

International Economics, *China: The Balance Sheet, What the World Needs to Know Now About the Emerging Superpower* (New York: Public Affairs, 2006).

5. A particularly assertive statement of this claim and of China's right to be left alone by the Western powers is to be found in Ma Zhengang, "China's Responsibility and the 'China Responsibility' Theory," *China International Studies*, no. 7 (Summer 2007).

4. THE WEST ON TRIAL

1. On this topic see Jeffrey Kopstein and Sven Steinmo, eds., *Growing Apart? America and Europe in the Twenty-first Century* (Cambridge: Cambridge University Press, 2008).

2. Emmanuel Todd, *After the Empire: The Breakdown of the American Order* (New York: Columbia University Press, 2003).

3. Zbigniew Brzezinski, *The Choice: Global Domination or Global Leadership* (New York: Basic, 2004).

4. On this return of sovereignism, see the stimulating essay by Pierre Manent, *La raison des nations: Réflexions sur la démocratie en Europe* (Paris: Gallimard, 2006).

5. For a survey of possible paths to relaunch Europe, see the report by Michel Foucher, *L'Union européenne un demi-siècle plus tard: État des lieux et scénarios de relance* (Paris: Fondation Robert Schuman, November 2006).

6. See along those lines, *The New Global Puzzle: What World for the EU in 2025?* (Paris: EU Institute for Security Studieis, 2006).

5. THE WEAPONS OF PEACE

The title of this chapter is derived from a book by Samuel Pisar, an international lawyer who, in the midst of the cold war, extolled the peaceful virtues of trade between East and West. Nowadays, however, globalization is not enough to foster peace and may even work against it.

1. World Bank, *Global Economic Prospects: Managing the Next Wave of Globalization* (Washington, DC: World Bank, 2007).

2. "Common Query: How Many Immigrants Can Be Absorbed?" *International Herald Tribune*, June 29, 2006.

3. Joseph P. Quinlan, *Drifting Apart or Growing Together? The Primacy of the Transatlantic Economy* (Washington, DC: Center for Transatlantic Relations, 2003).

4. Richard Youngs, *Europe's Flawed Approach to Arab Democracy* (London: Center for European Reform, 2006).

5. World Bank, *Africa Development Indicators* (Washington, DC: World Bank, 2006).

6. Nicholas Stern, *The Economics of Climate Change* (London: Cambridge University Press, 2006).

7. FAO, *Evaluation of World Food Security* (Rome: FAO, 2006).

8. Robert Kagan, "Power and Weakness," *Policy Review* , no. 113 (June-July 2002).

INDEX

Abu Dhabi Investment Authority, 23
Abu Ghraib prison, 33, 40
Afghanistan, 8; as "failed" state, 9;
    stabilizing, 111, 114; Sunni Islamist
    movement, 9
AIDS, 96, 107, 109
"American decline," 27
"American Empire," 3
Anti-Americanism, 33–34, 78, 83
"Arab street," 60
Arab-Muslim world, 59, 75; democracy
    and, 104–6; globalization and, 104–5;
    immigration, 11; isolation in, 100;
    "neighborhood policy," 105; stagna-
    tion of, 93; see also Islam
Atlantic era: asymmetrical decline,
    46–49; backlash, 29–32; democratic
    recession, 39–42; end of, 27–29;
    multilateralism crisis, 35–39; pillars
    of, 30–31; return of empires, 56–58;
    rift, 73; shifting brain power, 42–46;
    solidarity in, 30; twilight of pax
    Americana, 33–35

Atlantic solidarity, 80; priorities for,
    102–10; renewal of, 83; toward new
    pact, 110–14
Authoritarianism, 14

Barcelona Process, 106
Beijing-Teheran energy axis, 21
Berlin Wall, 1, 7, 32, 51, 88
Bipolar world, 1, 7; beginnings, 29; end
    of, 73; as stable, 54
Blair, Tony, 40
Bolivia, 20
Brain power: shifting east, 42–46; Unit-
    ed States, 48
Brazil, 5, 13, 57; "Brazilian model," 20;
    as continental nation, 14; economy
    of, 19–20; as "world's farm," 20
Brazil, Russia, India, China study
    (BRIC study), 13
"Breakdown of American order," 82
Bretton Woods, 36
BRIC study; see Brazil, Russia, India,
    China study

Bush, George W., 2, 40, 74, 81; Iraq intervention, 34; United States of, 35; war on Islamist terror, 10

Capitalism, 5; global, 23; new, in emerging countries, 25
China, 5; as continental nation, 14; dependence on outside world, 69; as developing country, 65–66; economic growth, 6, 12, 13; energy consumption, 22–23; foreign exchange reserves, 16; GDP, 16, 28; human capital, 16; on international stage, 2; leadership, 117; military budget, 68; "peaceful rise" doctrine, 65; population, 14–15; purchasing power, 116; R&D investment, 16; rising power of, xiii, 15, 44, 55, 93–94; Russia partnership, 71; shift to modernization, 6; United States and, 69–70; as unknown, 64–72; "workshop of the world," 15
Chirac, Jacques, 40, 79
Civil wars, xii, 4
"Clash of civilizations," 11, 52–53
"Coalitions of the willing," 35
Cold war: end of, xi, 30; simplicity of, xii; see also Post–cold war era
Common good, xii; Western democracies' influence for, 4
Communism, 2, 14
"Concert of nations," 104
Conflicts: changing nature of, xii; Israel-Palestinian, 2; Muslim/West, 5, 7; see also East/West conflicts; Global conflicts
"Cultural imperialism," 46

"De-Americanization," 46

Delors, Jacques, 91
Democracy, 40; Arab-Muslim world and, 104–5; blows to, 55; "global," 24; United States as decentralized, 47; see also Western democracies
Democratic recession, 39–42
Diplomacy, 54

East/West conflicts: areas of, 10–11; global confrontation, 11; new, 8–12; new antagonism, 9; roots of, 8
Economic integration, 4
Economy, 29, 45; of Brazil, 19–20; of China, 6, 12, 13; of emerging countries, 23–24, 43; of India, 12, 13; market, 41, 42; of Russia, 18; see also Gross Domestic Product
EEC; see European Economic Community
Emerging countries: economies of, 23–24, 43; GDP of, 13; influence of, 29; international order role, 101–2; new capitalism, 25; population increase, 28; revolution of, 12–20; rise of, 27; on world stage, 115; see also Brazil; China; India; Russia
Empires: old, 58; return of, 56–58
"End of history" theory, 51
Energy consumption: China, 22–23; EU, 21; United States, 21
Energy sources: control of, 93; fossil fuels, 109; world competition for, 22
Engagement, 55
Enlightenment, 100
EU; see European Union
Eurasia, 64, 114
Europe: decline, 29; end of, 87–92; "Greater Europe," 32; integration, 83; job losses, 42; multilateralism

and, 90; multipolar world and, 79–80; trading power, 29; unification, 30; United States and, 81–82; *see also* "Other Europe"

European Constitution, 32

European Council, 90

European Economic Community (EEC), 31

European Single Market, 98

European unification, xi, 1–2, 32, 40; pillars of, 88

European Union (EU), 56; acknowledging United States, 113–14; avoiding global conflicts, 93; Common Agricultural Policy, 37; disagreements, 32; energy consumption, 21; establishment, 31; external policy, 114; gas purchase, 19, 63; growth rate, 47; leadership, 116–17; military intervention, 112; preserving influence, 89; rejection of, 3; as "sentinel of liberty," 99; stumbling of, 87

Europeanization, 29

Extremism, 5, 39

FAO; *see* Food and Agriculture Organization

Food and Agriculture Organization (FAO), 103

Fragmentation, 4

France, 28

Free market, 25; globalization, 36

"Free world," xii

Friedman, Tom, 4

Fukuyama, Francis, 51, 53

Fundamentalism: growth of, 2; modernity and, 9; movements, 10; nationalism and, 4; Shiite, 8; terrorism and, 81

FWP; *see* World Food Program

G7, 19, 29, 35, 38

G20, 37, 57

GATT; *see* General Agreements on Tariffs and Trade

Gazprom, 19, 43

GDP; *see* Gross Domestic Product

General Agreements on Tariffs and Trade (GATT), 29, 36

Geopolitical paradigm, 6, 24

Germany, 12

Global Attitudes Survey, 33

Global conflicts, 93; EU avoiding, 93; rising dangers of, 93–96; United States avoiding, 93

Global governance, 52

Global reshaping, xii

Global warming: attenuating, 95; effects, 96; reducing, 108–10; in sub-Saharan Africa, 96; victims, 96

Globalization, xi–xii; acceleration, 116; "American," 7; Arab-Muslim world and, 104–6; "flattened," 4, 53; as flourishing, 7; free market, 36; geopolitical effects of, 25–26, 71; governance and, 104; increasing tensions, 24; international system driving force, 3–4; Islam and, 7; new face of, 5–6; of R&D, 45; terrorism and, 119n2; United States as champion, 85–86; on wire, 21–26

"Greater Europe," 32

Gross Domestic Product (GDP), 13; China, 16, 28; India, 17, 28; Russia, 19; United States, 28

Guantanamo prison, 33, 40, 76

Hamas, 11

Hezbollah, 60, 71, 81
History: "end of history" theory, 51; return of, 6–8
Honor, 15
Hu Jinato, 18
Human capital: China, 16; India, 45
Human rights, 41
Huntington, Samuel, 52, 53
Hussein, Saddam, 11, 75, 76
Hyperterrorism, 77

IAEA; see International Atomic Energy Agency
Identity, 3
IFAD; see International Fund for Agricultural Development
IMF; see International Monetary Fund
Immigration, 28, 92; Muslim, 11; political/humanitarian challenges, 97–99
India, 3, 5, 13; as continental nation, 14; GDP, 17, 28; growth, 6, 13, 17–18; human capital, 45; as major economic player, 12, 13; power position of, 6; "shining," 17; United States agreement, 57
Industrialized countries: demographic marginalization, 28; influence of, 29; population decline, 28
International Atomic Energy Agency (IAEA), 60, 103
International Fund for Agricultural Development (IFAD), 103
International Monetary Fund (IMF), 17, 29, 104
International relations, xi
Internet: bubble, 47; revolution, 2
Iran, 54; determination, 58; global security and, 59–62; Islamic Republic, 8; Islamic revolution, 6; nuclear pro-

gram, 59, 95; power of, 61; stabilizing, 111–12; threat from, 58–62
Iraq: invasion, xi; justifying intervention, 34; opposition to invading, 77; stabilizing, 111; Sunni domination weakened, 59; United States failure in, 3, 32, 33
Iron curtain, 1
Islam: globalization and, 7; Islamism vs., 12, 107; modern nationalism, 106; radical, 2, 5, 9; revival in, 107; see also Arab-Muslim world
Islamism, 12, 107
Isolationism, 86, 90
Israel-Palestinian conflict, 2, 81

Japan: military budget, 68; rearmament, 60
Al Jazeera, 41
Jihad, 5

Khomeini, Ayatollah, 8
Kissinger, Henry, 84
Kuwait Investment Authority, 23
Kyoto Protocol, 109

Liberal reformism, 40
Liberalism, 3
Libya, 55

Malnutrition, 95–96, 109–10
Mao Zedong, 68
Market economy, 41, 42
Marshall Plan, 106–7
Mexico, 57
Middle East: domination of, 93–94; "New Middle East," 55; as "world's powder keg," 62
Middle Kingdom, 64

Monnet, Jean, 31
Multilateralism, 3, 4; crisis, 35–39; decline of, 87–88; Europe and, 90; nationalism and, 38–39; United States, 80
Multipolar world, 1; advent of, 57, 102; as chaos, 53–54; Europe's interest in, 79–80
Muslim/West conflicts, 5, 7

National Bureau of Economic Research, 45
Nationalism, 3, 4; fundamentalism and, 4; modern Islamic, 106; multilateralism and, 38–39
"Neighborhood policy," 105
"New economy," 2
"New international order," 2
"New Middle East," 55
NGOs; see Nongovernmental organizations
Nixon, Richard, 64
Nongovernmental organizations (NGOs), 110
Nonstate actors, xii
Non-Western actors, 6
North Atlantic Treaty Organization (NATO), 30, 52; capacity extended, 112
North Korea, 38, 54
NPT; see Nuclear nonproliferation treaty
Nuclear nonproliferation treaty (NPT), 38
Nuclear proliferation, 4
Nye, Joseph, 84

OECD; see Organisation for Economic Cooperation and Development

Oil shock (1973), 7
Old Continent, 11
Organisation for Economic Cooperation and Development (OECD), 16, 29, 44
Oslo peace process, 9
"Other Europe," 31
Outsourcing, 42

Pakistan, 9
Palestine, 11
Paris-Berlin-Moscow axis, 77–78
Peaceful homogenization, xi
"Peaceful rise" doctrine, 65
Population: China, 14–15; decline in industrialized countries, 28; emerging countries' increase, 28
Populism, 39
Post–cold war era, 1, 3; paradigm controversy in, 51; "politically correct" visions of, 41
Protectionism, 25, 78
Putin, Vladimir, 14, 19, 22, 56; policies, 64; popularity, 62

Al-Qaeda, 8, 9, 60, 75

R&D; see Research and Development
Realism, 52
Red Army, 8
Religious revival, 7
Research and Development (R&D): China investment, 16; globalization of, 45; United States investment, 44
Rosneft, 43
Russia, 13; ambitions of, 56–57; China partnership, 71; as continental nation, 14; democratization of, 2–3; economic growth, 18; in G7, 19;

Russia (*continued*)
GDP, 19; at heart of Eurasia, 64;
leadership, 117; military budget, 68;
return to international stage, 62–64;
United States partnership, 56

Sachs, Jeffrey, 107
Saudi Arabia, 9
Saudi Arabia Investment Fund, 23
Schuman, Robert, 31
SCO; *see* Shanghai Cooperation Orga-
nization
"Sentinel of liberty," 99
September 11 terrorist attacks, xi, 2, 7, 8
Shanghai Cooperation Organization
(SCO), 71
Shiites: fundamentalists, 8; "Shiite
arc," 60
"Single Market" project, 91
Sino-American duopoly, 49, 72
Solidarity: in Atlantic era, 30; transat-
lantic, 116; *see also* Atlantic solidar-
ity; Western solidarity
Somalia, 9
South Africa, 57
South Korea, 57
"Southern pole," 57
Soviet Union, 1, 9, 30
Sub-Saharan Africa: AIDS in, 107, 109;
global warming in, 96; malnutrition
in, 96; rescuing, 107
Sudan, 9
Sunni Islamist movement, 9

Tactical reconciliation, 80–84
Taliban, 8, 112–13
Terrorism, xi–xii, 4, 58–59, 83; Bush
declares war on Islamic, 10; fight
against, 12; fundamentalism and, 81;

globalization and, 119n2; hyperter-
rorism, 77; mass, 5; religious revival
vs., 7; root of, 8; *see also* September
11 terrorist attacks; "War against
terror"
Third world, 5
Totalitarianism, xii
Trade, 24, 29, 36, 45; liberalization of
world, 7; transatlantic free trade
zone, 93–94; *see also* World Trade
Organization
Transatlantic solidarity, 116
Trilateral Commission, 35
Turkey, 33

UN; *see* United Nations
UN Commission for Trade and Development (UNCTAD), 45
UNCTAD; *see* UN Commission for
Trade and Development
Unipolar American power, 1, 85
United Nations (UN), 29–30; Human
Rights Commission, 38; marginalization of, 35; new agencies for, 103
United States: acknowledging EU, 113–
14; arrogance, 34; Asian resources
threatening, 44; avoiding global conflicts, 93; brain power, 48; of Bush,
35; China and, 69–70; as decentralized democracy, 47; demographic
growth, 47–48; energy consumption, 21; Europe and, 81–82; GDP, 28;
as globalization champion, 85–86; as
"Great Satan," 9; India agreement,
57; innovation, 48; Iraq, failure in, 3,
32, 33; job losses, 42; leadership, 83,
86, 116–17; military budget, 68; military power, 48; multilateralism, 80;
R&D investment, 44; recovering re-

spect, 84–87, 112–13; rise to power, 12; Russia partnership, 56; as "sentinel of liberty," 99; tarnished prestige, 76–77; trading power, 29; unilateralism, 78; see also "American decline"; "American Empire"; Anti-Americanism; "Breakdown of American order"; "De-Americanization"; Sino-American duopoly
UN Security Council: confronting new disorders, 103; monopolizing, 102; reform, 102–3; strengthening, 103

Valley of the Wolves Iraq, 33
Venezuela, 20

"War against terror," 33; decreasing emphasis, 116; failures of, 41; global, 75–76
"Washington consensus," 36
Western democracies, xii; common good influence, 4; leadership decline in, 26; victory of, 2
Western solidarity, 73; challenges to, 74–75; dangers of exclusive defensive, 99–100; narrow path of, 96–102
WFP; see World Food Program
WHO; see World Health Organization
"Workshop of the world," 15
World Bank, 29, 95
World Food Program (WFP), 103
World Health Organization (WHO), 103
World prices, 42
World Trade Organization (WTO), 2, 17; Cancun conference, 37; Doha round, 37, 104, 111; establishment, 36; failures, 36–37
World War II, 15, 29, 31, 35, 65, 74
"World's farm," 20
World's revolution, 12–20
WTO; see World Trade Organization

Yeltsin, Boris, 14, 18, 56